OVER *the* MOON

By Jodi Picoult & Jake van Leer

Music & Lyrics by
Ellen Wilber & Jodi Picoult

Simon Pulse
New York London Toronto Sydney

SIMON PULSE

An imprint of Simon & Schuster Children's Publishing Division

1230 Avenue of the Americas, New York, NY 10020

First Simon Pulse paperback edition January 2011

Text copyright © 2011 by Jodi Picoult and Jake van Leer

Music copyright © 2011 by Ellen Wilber

Lyrics copyright © 2011 by Jodi Picoult

Sticker art by Cara E. Petrus copyright © 2011 by Simon & Schuster, Inc.

All rights reserved, including the right of reproduction in whole or in part in any form.

SIMON PULSE and colophon are registered trademarks of Simon & Schuster, Inc.

For information about special discounts for bulk purchases, please contact
Simon & Schuster Special Sales at 1-866-506-1949 or business@simonandschuster.com.

The Simon & Schuster Speakers Bureau can bring authors to your live event.
For more information or to book an event contact the Simon & Schuster Speakers Bureau
at 1-866-248-3049 or visit our website at www.simonspeakers.com.

Designed by Mike Rosamilia

The text of this book was set in Prestige Elite.

Manufactured in the United States of America

2 4 6 8 10 9 7 5 3

Library of Congress Control Number 2010933585

ISBN 978-1-4424-2132-5

ISBN 978-1-4424-2133-2 (eBook)

Special thanks to transcriptionist Dan Cragan

INFORMATION ON PERFORMING THIS PLAY

I am fourteen years old and the boy sitting opposite me is feeding me marbles. "The rain in Spain," I say, in a thick Cockney accent, "stays mainly in the plain." I am Eliza Doolittle for the next two hours, and a few scenes later when I reappear, elegant, wearing a bottle-green velvet gown, I hear the collective gasp of the audience.

When I was growing up, theater was a big part of my life. It gave me a chance to be someone I wasn't; it taught me how to succeed at public speaking; it gave me an instant group of friends. My very first kiss, in fact, came from a boy playing the Artful Dodger in a production of *Oliver!* So perhaps it isn't surprising that when my own kids were in middle school, I wanted them to have the same experience I did onstage. The only problem? The theater program in their school didn't offer many opportunities. My solution? To create my own theater program instead. I wrote a short play that was fun and funny and age-appropriate—and that play, unlike most of my novels, actually had a happy ending. My children were too young at the time to read my books, and this was a way to share my writing with them.

The Trumbull Hall Troupe was born with ten kids on a tiny stage in a community hall attached to a local church. A friend, Marjorie Rose, was our director. Our modus operandi was twofold: to raise money for charity so that our kids realized that even at a young age they could make a difference in the world, and to provide a theater experience to the kids who might otherwise be crushed by a traditional audition process—those who were quiet, or who had no stage experience. If you were invited to be in the troupe, you had a part, and that was that. The father of one cast member could play Beatles songs on the guitar, so I rewrote the lyrics to some of those songs and peppered the play with them. We teamed up with the Zienzele Foundation, a group that provides help to HIV/AIDS orphans in Zimbabwe. The kids over there became pen pals with our cast, so there was an immediate and real connection that the work they were doing onstage was benefiting children half a world away.

To say our theater program experiment was successful would be an understatement. As the program grew, so did the production staff. My son, Jake van Leer, began cowriting the plays, which grew more complex and accommodated larger casts. My friend Ellen Wilber, a veteran musical performer and longtime music teacher, came on board to write original music for the plays and to serve as music director. Alexandra Lovejoy and I started codirecting the shows, and Allyson Weiner Sawyer became our choreographer. We began working with Dan Cragan to transcribe the music. We quickly outgrew our space and moved our performance venue to the middle school auditorium. Now, seven years into it, the Trumbull Hall Troupe has forty kids performing onstage and working behind the scenes. Ellen and I have written the music and lyrics to more than one hundred songs. Our plays have raised more than forty thousand dollars for charity. And yet our mission is still the same: to create an original musical that can be performed by kids ages twelve to eighteen (many of whom are on a stage for the first time), the ticket revenue from which is used to benefit children whose lives are less fortunate than the troupe's own.

I have heard from many drama teachers who bemoan the fact that their kids perform the same old chestnuts over and over, that few are really age appropriate, and that only a limited number of musicals accommodates a good-sized cast. *Over the Moon* is the antidote to those problems. In the spirit of inclusiveness, we have a tradition at the troupe of awarding stickers at the end of each rehearsal to three kids who have worked exceptionally hard. You'd think that high school kids would scoff at the thought of receiving a princess sticker, but they loved it (so much so that they'd yell at us if we forgot to give out the stickers at the end of rehearsal), and their scripts became dotted with the proof of positive feedback. We've provided stickers here, just in case you'd like to incorporate this tradition into your own theater program.

I am proud of how far the Trumbull Hall Troupe has come, and of the money we've raised for charity—but most of all, I'm struck by the tools we have given our cast members to carry with them through the rest of their lives. I've watched the ease our cast members have when it comes to speaking in public; I've seen children who were quiet as mice get up two years later and belt out a song; I've watched shy kids shrug themselves into a character and become someone completely different. I've witnessed upperclassmen mentoring underclassmen; I've seen how kids from different school districts learn how to collaborate instead of compete. I have watched kids take risks and exceed even their own expectations. The most magical thing happens in drama: By trying on another persona for size, these young actors learn more about themselves.

It has been thirty years since I played Eliza Doolittle, but if you beg me, I can still sing "Wouldn't It Be Loverly" in a full-out Cockney accent. Every time I speak at a book signing, I am reminded of the first time I stepped onstage as a teenager, heart pounding, and looked out at an audience. I loved musical theater then, and I love it now, because drama brings back that childhood moment when the world is full of possibility and you can be anything and anyone you want. It's no coincidence that the art form you'll see here is called a "play." To that end, I believe that theater for kids should be fun, energetic, and enjoyable. But I also believe Shakespeare when he wrote "all the world's a stage." What if a silly fractured fairy tale does not just entertain, but makes one shy kid who's watching think, *I'd like to be a part of that one day*? What if the message in *Over the Moon*—to be yourself and be proud of it—is absorbed by the audience and taken back into the real world? Frankly, I cannot think of a better way for life to imitate art.

Jodi Picoult

August 2010

CAST (IN ORDER OF APPEARANCE)

Hairy Godmother	A hairy, masculine godmother; narrator
Johnny Nova	Radio show host
Stella	A star, and friend to Luna
Bella	A star, and friend to Luna
Luna	The moon; disguised as a boy named Leo when in Hanoveria; in love with Prince Jack
Newsboy	Newspaper salesperson in the town
Baker	Baker in the town
Fishmonger	Fishmonger in the town
Flower Lady	Flower lady in the town
Butcher	Butcher in the town
Ferocia	Queen of Hanoveria, sister of Hugo
Gertrude	Princess of Hanoveria, daughter of Ferocia
Eunice	Princess of Hanoveria, daughter of Ferocia
Felicity	A young lady of noble birth who is a bit of a tomboy; smitten with Leo
Prince Jack	Prince of Hanoveria, nephew of Ferocia and son of Hugo; in love with Felicity
Mama Bear	Bear who lives with Papa Bear, Baby Bear, Jean-Claude, and Hugo
Papa Bear	Bear on the outskirts of Hanoveria
Baby Bear	Bear on the outskirts of Hanoveria
Jean-Claude	Servant to Hugo; was cast out of Hanoveria
Hugo	King of Hanoveria; was cast out after Ferocia's spell turned him into a giant

Pinocchio	A wooden puppet, servant to Ferocia
Cinderella	A princess married to Prince Charming
Grumpy	Son of Snow White
Sneezy	Daughter of Snow White
Snow White	A princess married to a different Prince Charming
Sleeping Beauty	A princess with narcolepsy, married to a prince
Tree 1	A talking tree in the Enchanted Forest
Tree 2	A talking tree in the Enchanted Forest
Humpty Dumpty	A big egg traveling the country on a Harley
Wolves	Wolves of Hanoveria that attack Felicity
Li'l Red From The Hood	Young hip-hop girl; interested in Jack
Goldilocks	Young girl with blond hair; interested in Jack
Old Woman Who Lives In A Shoe	Older woman; interested in Jack
Porky	One of three pigs; construction worker
Hamlet	One of three pigs; construction worker
Francis Bacon	One of three pigs; construction worker
Blitzer	Wolf who is foreman of a construction company
Rapunzel	Girl who escapes from her tower
Prince Sheldon	Prince who was supposed to rescue Rapunzel from her tower
Mickey	One of three blind mice
Minnie	One of three blind mice
Algernon	One of three blind mice

ACT ONE

SCENE 1

A cross-dressed HAIRY GODMOTHER enters, holding a book.

> HAIRY GODMOTHER
> (opening book)
> Once upon a time...
> (beat)
> What? What's the matter? You've never
> seen a hairy godmother before?
> (beat)
> Maybe you were expecting someone --
> a little different? Someone with a
> little less testosterone? Some sweet
> old grandma type with a blue cloak
> and a magic wand? A FAIRY godmother?
> (beat)
> Well, news flash: that was a TYPO!
> (beat)
> You can't believe everything you
> read in fairy tales. Jack and the
> magic beanstalk? We're talking
> genetically modified plants, here.
> And the three little pigs? They
> went on to become [Insert name of
> local development company].
> (beat)
> I hear what you're saying: the whole
> point of a fairy tale is that everyone
> knows the story. Sure as the moon's
> in the sky every night, Cinderella's
> always gonna lose her glass slipper
> and Rapunzel's always gonna have a
> grooming problem, and me, well, I'm
> gonna wave the wand around and sing
> "Bibbidi-Bobbidi-Boo."
> (beat)
> But what if the moon WASN'T in the
> sky? Because THAT'S a story I bet
> you've never heard...

He walks off, revealing:

SCENE 2

LUNA, the moon, and her friends, STELLA and BELLA, are up in
the sky, listening to the radio.

> JOHNNY NOVA
> Howdy folks, welcome back to the number
> one satellite radio show in the galaxy.
> I'm Johnny Nova, comin'at you so bright
> you better keep your shades on!

> STELLA
> Guys, guys! It's on again!!!

> JOHNNY NOVA
> Now, let's get back to some of those
> hit Nep-Tunes...

> STELLA
> Hey, Bella, does this dress make my
> asteroid look fat?

> BELLA
> Honestly, Stella, you KNOW you're a
> heavenly body.

> LUNA
> People down there just don't get it!

> STELLA
> Don't tell me you're spying again.

> BELLA
> Oh, stop being such a blue moon!
> Humans mess everything up.

> LUNA
> Seeing them throw away love makes me
> want to just stop glowing! Seriously,
> girls, why else are we here?

Bella and Stella look at each other and shrug.

> BELLA
> The universal health care plan?

> LUNA
> No! All those wishes on a falling
> star. All those kisses in the
> moonlight. But each night I see
> humans throwing away true love.

SONG 1: OVER THE MOON

LUNA:

When it comes to love, you shoot for the stars.

When it comes to love, no journey's too far.

Love is worth waiting for.

Love conquers all

right from the moment you fall.

LUNA WITH STELLA AND BELLA:

Someday I will find the guy of my dreams.

Someday I will find a fella who seems

like he was meant for me,

a perfect pair,

and then a lifetime we'll share!

CHORUS:

Every word he whispers

is a secret tune.

Every one of his kisses, I know,

will send me over the moon!

Maybe one day I will walk down a street,

and, by chance, our eyes will happen to meet.

And we will know right then

we're meant to be,

forever after happily!

And we will know right then

we're meant to be,

forever after happily!

> JOHNNY NOVA
> This one's going out to all you
> lovers...

> LUNA
> That's it! Girls, I'm leaving. If
> people on Earth can't find true love,
> I'm going to find it for them!

SCENE 3: Side of stage

> HAIRY GODMOTHER
> And when the moon climbed down from
> the sky, she landed smack in the
> middle of the kingdom of Hanoveria...

> LUNA
> Excuse me, are you talking to me?

                    HAIRY GODMOTHER
Depends. Do you need a hairy
godmother?

                         LUNA
I thought it was a fair-

                    HAIRY GODMOTHER
It's a typo!
        (beat)
And besides, it wasn't that long ago
a certain someone had a crater face...

                         LUNA
Ok, ok. I had a little acne problem...

                    HAIRY GODMOTHER
You may want to think about your
looks again. Because if you're
planning to mingle with the masses,
you shouldn't...glow...quite so much.

Luna gasps and hides behind scenery as the town awakens.

SCENE 4: FULL CAST mingles in Hanoveria

SONG 2: WONDERFUL MORNING

                         NEWSBOY
         GOOD MORNING HANOVERIA!!!

ALL:

It's a wonderful morning.

It's gonna be a wonderful day.

Stop and chat with a friend,

or watch the world pass by from a café.

See the beautiful scenery.

Smell the fresh air and take a deep breath.

Best town ever to live in

'cept for the threat of sudden death!

CHORUS:

Guess it's true that life can change in the blink of an eye.

I love living here, but don't wanna die!

                    NEWSBOY (CONT'D)
          Get your copy of the Hanoveria
          [Insert name of local paper,
          i.e. Times, Globe, Courant] here!
          Pied Piper's house seized
          by the Department of Health!

LUNA:

Could it really be true?

Could I finally be down here at last?

What if somebody sees me?

Better disguise myself very fast.

Here's a basket of laundry.

I'll take some clothes and they'll never know.

How to act like a human;

maybe I start out with "hello"?

(She dresses herself up as a boy)

ALL:

Guess it's true that life can change in the blink of an eye.

We love living here. Can't you see why?

> BAKER
> (to fishmonger)
> Have you got a little smelt left?

> FISHMONGER
> I saved you some!

> LUNA
> (to baker)
> I think she likes you!

(They look at her like she's crazy)

> FLOWER LADY
> (to butcher)
> Any ribs today?

> BUTCHER
> I'm afraid not -- the giant let the cattle
> out of the pen and slaughtered them all!

> FLOWER LADY
> Better them than us! Well, maybe tomorrow.

ALL:

If you move here, you'll love it,

for there is just one tiny letdown.

There's a bloodthirsty giant

who's settled on the outskirts of town.

He might slaughter your chickens,

knock down your cottage, kidnap a waif.

Lucky we've got a queen who'll

do what it takes to keep us safe!

                    NEWSBOY
          Hey Diddle Diddle! Dish indicted for
          kidnapping spoon! Read all about it!
               (beat)
          It's her Majesty!!!

(FEROCIA enters trailed by GERTRUDE and EUNICE)

FEROCIA:

To all of Hanoveria,

I know you live in fear-ia,

but let me make it clear-ia.

I feel your pain.

And on this very solemn day,

let each of us make sure to say

the former king, my brother,

did not die in vain.

For when the giant came for him

and tore him up from limb to limb,

he saw the future looking grim

and intervened.

He called me on the verge of death

and told me with his dying breath

I must survive him nonetheless.

ALL:

Long live the queen.

Guess it's true that life can change in the blink of an eye.

We love living here. Can't you see why?

                    NEWSBOY (CONT'D)
          Extra! Extra! Gay marriage law
          passes! Butcher, baker, and
          candlestick maker give it a thumbs-up!

ALL:

U.S. News did its ranking.

We nabbed the highest spot of them all.

Just one small bit of trouble,

and it is standing ten feet tall.

So we keep up pretenses,

and we remember always to smile.

If the giant returns, well,

hope that it won't be for a while!

Guess it's true that life can change in the blink of an eye.

We love living here. Can't you see why?

Can't you see why?

At close of song, cast mills about.

                        GERTRUDE
        Mama, isn't it true that WE have
        nothing to worry about?

                        EUNICE
        Royalty like us gives giants
        indigestion.

                        GERTRUDE
        Our crowns get stuck in their teeth.

                        EUNICE
        Well, I heard the giant hates everyone,
        and everything about Hanoveria.

                        FEROCIA
        No, darling. That's [Insert name of
        local rabble-rouser in news].

They exit. Luna is in Ferocia's path. Ferocia clears her throat,
and Luna backs away.

FELICITY hurries across the stage, PRINCE JACK in pursuit.

                        FELICITY
        Wow!
            (feigning interest)
        A chicken can't swallow upside down?
        That is absolutely fascinating, Jack!

                        PRINCE JACK
        You...uh...y-you really think so?

                        FELICITY
        No! All I think about is YOU leaving
        ME alone!

She walks off. Jack follows, bumping Luna, who's lovestruck.

                        LUNA
        I...I'm sorry!

                         PRINCE JACK
              Boys will be boys, right?

                            LUNA
              Oh! But I'm not...

Jack's cousins hurry forward, arguing.

                           EUNICE
              Gosh, Jack, could you be any slower?

                          GERTRUDE
              He probably was talking to some girl.

                           EUNICE
                   (imitating Jack)
              Um, uh...d-do you know that a cow's
              sweat glands are in its nose?

                          GERTRUDE
              Nice pickup lines, Jack.

                           EUNICE
              The only girl you're gonna impress
              is Alex Trebek.

They exit.

                         PRINCE JACK
                   (to Luna)
              Be careful out there.

He smiles and exits.

                            LUNA
              Jack.
                   (to the fishmonger)
              Do you know that man?

                         FISHMONGER
              Everyone knows him, boy. That's the
              crown prince.

SONG 3: WONDERFUL MORNING (Reprise)

ALL:

It's a wonderful morning.

It's gonna be a wonderful day.

Stop and chat with a friend,

or watch the world pass by from a café.

THE SONG IS INTERRUPTED as HUGO, the giant, enters. Everyone screams and scatters offstage. Hugo, left alone, picks up a baguette and leaves. Everyone comes out of hiding, slowly picking up the verse again.

See the beautiful scenery.

Smell the fresh air and take a deep breath.

Best town ever to live in

'cept for the threat of sudden death!

Guess it's true that life can change in the blink of an eye.

We love living here. Can't you see why?

Can't you see why?

SCENE 5: The bear cave

Hairy Godmother appears on the side of the stage.

> HAIRY GODMOTHER
> The giant had been terrorizing the
> citizens of Hanoveria for 15 years --
> ever since Ferocia took over the
> kingdom. Coincidence? I think not.
> But then again, in a fairy tale,
> nothing's ever what it seems to be.
> (MORE)

HAIRY GODMOTHER (CONT'D)
Take a look for yourself.
(He waves his magic
wand; nothing happens)
Oh, for Pete's sake. I need some
double A batteries, people!

As he walks off, the scene opens. JEAN-CLAUDE, a servant,
sits with MAMA BEAR, PAPA BEAR, and BABY BEAR watching TV.
We "see" their program on the side of the stage, complete
with a mini rap performance by LI'L RED FROM THE HOOD.

JOHNNY NOVA
Welcome back to Hanoveria Idol! You
just heard Li'l Red From The Hood,
rapping "Grandma Got Run Over By a
Reindeer." Remember, if you want
Li'l Red to stay in the competition,
you have to vote!

MAMA BEAR
I think her voice was too high.

PAPA BEAR
Are you kidding me? It was too low.

BABY BEAR
I think it was JUUUUUUST right!

JEAN-CLAUDE
(pacing)
Hugo's been gone so long...

MAMA BEAR
Jean-Claude, you're too anxious.

PAPA BEAR
Well, I think he's too laid-back.

BABY BEAR
I think he's JUUUUUUUST right!

                         JEAN-CLAUDE
              Not a day goes by that I don't give
              thanks for your generosity, *mes amis*.
              You took us in when we were outcasts.
              And yet, a part of me wishes that...

There is a commotion as the giant enters, holding a baguette.
He is clearly rattled.

                      JEAN-CLAUDE (CONT'D)
              Master Hugo! You're finally back!

                         HUGO
              Jean-Claude, it was brutal out there.
              They treat me like...like I work for
              FairPoint [or name of local telephone
              or cable company]!
                   (beat)
              It was all I could do to snatch a
              loaf of bread.

                       MAMA BEAR
              I hope it's sourdough.

                       PAPA BEAR
              I hope it's rye.

                       BABY BEAR
              I hope it's gluten free!

                      JEAN-CLAUDE
              I hate to say I told you so, Master
              Hugo...but I...

                         HUGO
              DON'T SAY IT!

                      JEAN-CLAUDE
              I told --

                         HUGO
              Zip it!

                    JEAN-CLAUDE
          I --

Hugo growls menacingly, and Jean-Claude backs off.

                    JEAN-CLAUDE (CONT'D)
               (in a high, rushed
               voice)
          I told you so!

                    HUGO
          Look at me! I'm a giant. A freak.

                    JEAN-CLAUDE
          That's not true. If it weren't for
          Ferocia's spell you'd still be --

                    HUGO
          DO NOT MENTION THAT EVIL WITCH!

                    MAMA BEAR
          SOMEONE woke up on the wrong side of
          the bed this morning.

                    HUGO
          Someone doesn't even FIT on the bed.

                    MAMA BEAR
          It is a bit small.

                    PAPA BEAR
          You think? Feels pretty roomy to me.

                    BABY BEAR
          Well, I think it's...
               (beat)
          ...Just a matter of finding the
          right sleep number. Personally,
          I'm a 45. Firm, with just a hint
          of softness at the top of the
          mattress.

                    HUGO
Shouldn't you be hibernating?

                  MAMA BEAR
I knew it wasn't a good idea to
rent out the back room, especially
after the last boarder broke the
furniture.

                  PAPA BEAR
Do I need to remind you that we got
soaked last year in the stock market?
I told you we should have been more
bearish, honey.

                  BABY BEAR
Honey? Where?

They all run offstage.

                    HUGO
I don't know why I keep trying. I
should just go...find a foreclosed
beanstalk somewhere.

                  JEAN-CLAUDE
You keep trying because you know
that the spell can be broken.
You heard, uh, She-Who-Won't-Be-
Named. All it takes is *un peu
de l'amour...*

                    HUGO
Jean-Claude. Come on. You were
born in CLEVELAND.
      (beat)
And where am I supposed to find true
love, looking like this?

SONG 4: SUPERSIZED

JEAN-CLAUDE:

Surely you've heard the story of Goliath,

knocked to his knees by a shorty with a stone.

You know what they say about a guy who's small of stature.

Maybe his ego is what's overgrown.

Who else can put the lightbulb in a streetlamp?

Who sets the star on a Christmas tree with ease?

If your head's up in the clouds,

who cares about the angry crowds?

Nothing they say can bring you to your knees.

If the words of some Neanderthal

make it harder to keep walking tall,

just kneel down and look 'em in the eyes.

Say you're supersized!

HUGO:

Don't know what joker said size doesn't matter,

but I can bet he wasn't eight foot ten.

Every night I lie in bed, my feet hang off the mattress.

Oh, what I'd give to make them fit again.

JEAN-CLAUDE:

Buddy, you'll show 'em bigger can be better.

If they don't listen, stomp on them like ants!

HUGO:

Not sure that's the way to win back friends and loyal subjects.

JEAN-CLAUDE:

Don't settle for the same old song and dance.

DANCE BREAK

BOTH:

It doesn't matter if you're tall or if you're tiny.

Make sure your spirits are always on the rise.

So dry your eyes.

Long as you tell yourself you're supersized!

HUGO: Woo yeah!

SCENE 6: Ferocia's castle

DURING SCENE CHANGE:

> NEWSBOY
> This just in: Tortoise beats Hare
> to win [Insert name of local road or
> bike race]!

Ferocia stalks inside and looks around.

> FEROCIA
> Hello! Can I get some attention here!!

PINOCCHIO hurries in.

                    PINOCCHIO
Sorry, your majesty. I
was...um...writing a sonnet about
your random acts of kindness.

His nose grows. Ferocia crosses her arms, not amused.

                    FEROCIA
Pinocchio. Who was fired from his
last job?

                    PINOCCHIO
Me, your majesty.

                    FEROCIA
For what?

                    PINOCCHIO
Lying on my résumé, your majesty.

                    FEROCIA
And who rescued you from becoming
parquet flooring?

                    PINOCCHIO
You, your majesty.

                    FEROCIA
THAT'S RIGHT! You're one fib away
from being a box of toothpicks.
    (beat)
Do I look like I'm getting sick,
Pinocchio?

                    PINOCCHIO
You're the picture of health.

His nose grows and he covers it with a kerchief.

FEROCIA

Must we start random drug testing
again?

PINOCCHIO

No, ma'am. I kicked the fertilizer
habit for good.

FEROCIA

Never mind. It's just that with
everyone talking today about my
brother, the former king, I started
to feel a little...unloved.

PINOCCHIO

Well, you DID cast the spell that
turned him into a giant.

FEROCIA

What was I SUPPOSED to do? He always
thought he was soooo big and
important. Larger than life. I
just...accentuated that.
     (beat)
Besides, the citizens don't know
what I did to my brother. They trust
me to keep them safe!

PINOCCHIO

They said the same thing about Bernie
Madoff.

FEROCIA

We've got something else to worry
about. For years I've selflessly
given my nephew a home, but now that
he's eighteen, he can take this
kingdom from me once he's married.
This kingdom I've built with terror
and fear...Oh, Pinocchio.
     (sighs)
It's not easy being mean.

SONG 5: QUEEN OF MEAN

FEROCIA:

When I was a girl not so long ago,

my brother and I had a spat.

My mother advised,

I apologized,

and then I set fire to his favorite cat.

They thought I would outgrow my nasty tricks,

But I went from evil to worse.

I cheat, and I lie. I make people cry.

Honey, it's true: bad girls finish first.

I'm a downpour at a wedding.

I'm the flu without the vaccine.

Attila the Hun

seems awfully fun

compared to the Queen of Mean.

If you're thirsty in the desert,

You can bet that I'm a saltine.

Cruella De Vil

was run-of-the-mill

compared to the Queen of Mean.

Some say I took my brother's kingdom.

I rather prefer the word "STOLE."

That crash that he had?

Well, golly, my bad!

But world domination's a lofty goal.

The citizens may never love me,

But I can still rule them with fear.

They'll do as I say,

or maybe one day,

It's possible that they might disappear.

I'm a rip along your nylons.

I'm a one-woman mujahideen.

Mussolini

was a weenie

compared to the Queen of Mean.

I'm the sip of milk that's sour.

I'm a platter of lima beans.

George Bush is a saint

who showed great restraint

compared to the Queen of Mean,

The Queen of (makes sassy face) Mean!

REPRISE:

My costume always sells out

each and every Halloween.

I bite and I bark.

I've mastered my snark

because I'm the Queen of Mean,

The Queen of (kicks Pinocchio) *MEAN!!!!*

Jack and Eunice and Gertrude enter, still bickering.

                    FEROCIA (CONT'D)
          Hello, my beautiful darlings.

                    PRINCE JACK
          Pinocchio, do I have any messages?

                    PINOCCHIO
          Yes: you could lose 30 pounds with
          the Oprah Diet Berry Shake. And the
          widow of a Nigerian tycoon needs you
          to get the millions of dollars that
          rightfully belong to her.

                    PRINCE JACK
          Nothing from Felicity?

                    GERTRUDE
          As IF, Jack.

                    EUNICE
          You LOOK at a girl and break out in
          hives...

                    PRINCE JACK
          That was an allergic reaction to
          pollen...

                    GERTRUDE
In DECEMBER?

                    FEROCIA
Honestly, Jack, dear, if you're
lonely, I can fix you up...

                    PRINCE JACK
No offense, Aunt Ferocia, but that
didn't work out so well last time.

                    FEROCIA
You shouldn't have taken her target
shooting!

                    PRINCE JACK
You should have told me my blind
date was actually BLIND!

                    EUNICE
Jack's in love with Felicity.

                    PINOCCHIO
HOO-ah!!! She's the kind of girl
who makes me glad I'm a real boy.

                    GERTRUDE
But every time he's near her, he
blubbers.

                    PINOCCHIO
        (panicked)
BLUBBERS? Is there a WHALE around?

                    PRINCE JACK
I don't actually blubber.
        (beat)
I don't say ANYTHING.
        (to Ferocia)
I wish my dad was still here, so I
could talk to him.

FEROCIA
Don't we all.

PRINCE JACK
I bet we'd do father-son stuff.
Like fishing. Tossing a ball around.

PINOCCHIO
        (dreamily)
Rubbing my back with a belt sander...
        (beat)
Oh. Maybe that was just MY dad...

FEROCIA
Jack, your father would say to let
Felicity see the real you!

PRINCE JACK
You...you really think so?
        (hugs her)
Thanks, Aunt Ferocia. What would I
do without you?

He runs off.

FEROCIA
I'm hoping you'll never find out.
MUAAAHHAHAHAHA!

SCENE 7: A meadow with cottage

DURING SCENE CHANGE, Newsboy crosses stage:

NEWSBOY
Extra! Extra! Search for the
gingerbread man's missing body
continues...He was last seen running
fast as he could...

Felicity sits on a rock, reading PRINCESS BEHAVIOR FOR DUMMIES
and drinking a Coke. A cottage is in the background.

FELICITY

How hard could this possibly be? I
taught myself multivariable calculus,
and when the carburetor on my Mustang
died, I fixed it myself.
          (beat)
Chapter 1: How to Act Like a Princess.
          (reads)
A princess never troubles her brain
with something as complex as
multivariable calculus, or soils her
hands with auto repair works.
          (to audience)
Uh-oh.
          (reads)
To the contrary, a princess is admired
by everyone around her. She is kind
and well-groomed.
          (She sniffs her armpit)
So far so good!
          (reads)
A princess must never stoop to chat
with dragons.
          (to audience, heartened)
I don't even SPEAK dragon!
          (reads)
A princess must have a dainty walk.
          (trips and falls)
Above all else, a princess must have
impeccable...
          (LOUD BURP)
Manners.
          (sighs)
Who am I kidding? Sure, I look like
princess material. But it's only a
matter of time before everyone
realizes I'd rather go out hunting
for ogres and four-wheeling than
doing needlepoint in an ivory tower.
The last thing I need is a guy who
wants the kind of girl who only exists
in fairy tales.

SONG 6: A GIRL LIKE ME

FELICITY:

Act like a lady.

Never use your mind.

Don't interrupt.

Always be kind.

Live your life as long as it's confined.

Beauty is a virtue,

but I must confess

underneath this pretty face,

I am still a mess.

Where's the guy who wants a girl like me?

I prefer a hiking boot

to any dancing shoe.

I can climb the Matterhorn

Or dabble in kung fu.

I can hawk a loogie

And use a power tool,

But I'll never graduate from finishing school.

Why does growing up mean I can't have fun?

I will tell myself there's got to be someone

whose happy endings match mine perfectly,

the kind of guy who wants a girl like me.

I may look the part,

But I'm no perfect lass.

I can belch the loudest.

Sometimes I have gas.

If I had the choice

I'd never wear a dress.

Skirts severely hamper

a full-court press.

Why does growing up mean that I can't have fun?

I will tell myself there's got to be someone

whose happy endings match mine perfectly,

the kind of guy who wants a girl like me,

girl like me.

But until that day,

I will just pretend

that I could be

the perfect girlfriend,

though I know I'll be at my wit's end.

So I keep smiling,

and they'll never know

I can sink a basket

every time I throw.

Where's the guy who wants a girl like me?

Like me.

As she finishes, Prince Jack enters. Embarrassed, Felicity tries to cover up what she's been doing.

> FELICITY (CONT'D)
> Oh, uh, I was just doing my
> needlepoint exercises. We ladies
> have to keep ourselves fit, you know.

She does some ninja moves that mimic sewing.

> PRINCE JACK
> Well, you're very fit.
>> (stammers, blushing)
> I mean, you're the right size. Not
> too big. Not that I have a problem
> with a big girl. Which you're not.
> But you're not so small that you'd
> have to worry about getting lost in
> a crowd or sinking down a drain or...
>> (picks up her book)
> Could you just smack me in the head
> and put me out of my misery?

> FELICITY
> That's a trick question. Ladies never
> hit anything. Not even a mosquito.

> PRINCE JACK
>> (looking at book)
> What's this?

                    FELICITY
Gee, I don't know. A very flat,
rectangular monkey?

                    PRINCE JACK
You're the last person who'd need to
read about behaving like a princess...

                    FELICITY
        (grabbing it)
I'm really busy right now --

                    PRINCE JACK
I, um, came to ask you a question,
Lady Felicity...

                    FELICITY
Yes?

                    PRINCE JACK
I, well, would you...that is, could
you possibly...if you don't mind...

                    FELICITY
SPIT...IT....OUT...
        (gasps)
Except ladies never spit.
        (beat)
EXPECTORATE...IT...OUT...!

                    PRINCE JACK
I was wondering...uh...if...you...
        (closes his eyes)
Aregoingtofinishyoursoda.

                    FELICITY
What?

                    PRINCE JACK
        (grimacing)
I just asked if you...were going to
finish your soda.

She shakes her head and hands it to him.

> PRINCE JACK (CONT'D)
> I...guess I'll see you around.

He walks off with her Coke.

> FELICITY
> Thank goodness he's gone!

Out of the cottage comes CINDERELLA.

> CINDERELLA
> You can say that again, sister.

> FELICITY
> Don't I know you from somewhere?

> CINDERELLA
> Yeah. I get that a lot. But the
> first time you crack a glass slipper
> on the cobblestones you're sweeping,
> you start wearing Uggs instead.

> FELICITY
> You're Cinderella?

> CINDERELLA
> The one and only, sweetheart.

> FELICITY
> Oh! I thought you lived in a castle.
>   (sympathetic)
> Did Prince Charming work on Wall Street?

> CINDERELLA
> I WISH. I'd be happy if he worked
> AT ALL. Everyone knows my story,
> right? I got the prince in the end.
> And you know what else I got? A
> big spoiled brat who sits in his
>   (MORE)

>   CINDERELLA (CONT'D)
> Barcalounger all day long, watching
> unicorn races on ESPN. It's not
> so charming when he yells, "HEY,
> CINDY! CAN YOU BRING ME ANOTHER
> RED BULL?"
>   (beat)
> I thought I escaped from being my
> stepmother's maid, and I end up
> with a guy who makes an even bigger
> mess.
>   (beat)
> Oh. You've got a little schmutz on
> your nose. Here, let me...

She polishes Felicity's face as SNOW WHITE enters. She has
four babies in a Snugli and is holding the hands of two
children, GRUMPY and SNEEZY. She is hugely pregnant.

>   GRUMPY
> Mama, she started it. She took my
> pet frog out of its cage...

>   SNEEZY
> I...Ah-CHOO! Did not!

>   SNOW WHITE
> Sneezy, don't tell me you're coming
> down with another cold?
>   (beat)
> Cinderella, did you try to give
> Grumpy's pet frog a bath again?

>   CINDERELLA
> I have no recollection of that...

>   SNEEZY
> I saw her! And she put little Bashful
> through the dishwasher!

Snow White gasps and clutches one of the babies tighter.

                    CINDERELLA
Well, honestly! She gets so dirty,
crawling around on the floor...

                    SNOW WHITE
Hard to believe, given that Mrs. OCD
here mops it seven times a day...Ooooh,
kids, I think it's time for Dora!

Grumpy and Sneezy exit. She thrusts the babies at Felicity.

                SNOW WHITE (CONT'D)
Here, can you hold the rugrats for a
second? My back is killing me.

                    FELICITY
Snow White? But you're supposed to
be living happily ever after with
Prince Charming too...
        (gasps)
Wait! He's a polygamist!?

                    CINDERELLA
No, they're brothers. But someone
SHOULD have made that more clear.

                    SNOW WHITE
        (taking back her babies)
Charming? Oh, he's charming all
right. He's got the dreamiest blue
eyes and the cutest set of dimples,
and where did that get me? Six trips
to the [name of hospital] birthing
pavilion, and another one due any
minute. Just when I thought a guy had
rescued me from having seven little
people underfoot all the time...it turns
out that I'm the runner-up for the
Octomom. I've jumped right from the
frying pan into the fire.

SLEEPING BEAUTY runs out of the cottage, frantic.

                    SLEEPING BEAUTY
          Fire? Did someone yell fire?

                      CINDERELLA
          False alarm, Sleeping Beauty.

                    SLEEPING BEAUTY
          Oh, great. I was finally getting a
          little rest. Look at me! I'm a
          wreck. I've got bags under my eyes
          and my hands are shaking...

                       FELICITY
          What happened?

                    SLEEPING BEAUTY
          My husband, that's what. Everyone
          knows my story, but...

She nods off, snoring lightly.

                      CINDERELLA
          Narcolepsy.

Snow White pokes Sleeping Beauty, who wakes with a start.

                    SLEEPING BEAUTY
          McDreamy, honestly, you don't want
          Meredith...OH! I must have nodded
          off. Well, as I was saying -- the
          important details are always missing.
          Like the fact that I can't take a
          spinning class at the gym without
          hyperventilating. Or that the prince
          who woke me up in the fairy tale
          snores. Do you know how long it's
          been since I got a good night's sleep?

                      CINDERELLA
                    (to Felicity)
          Girl, if you know what's good for you,
                        (MORE)

                    CINDERELLA (CONT'D)
you'll make sure you're never close
enough for Prince Jack to even THINK
the word "MARRIAGE."

                    FELICITY
Oh, the last thing he'd ever want
is --

                    CINDERELLA
A free maid?

                    SNOW WHITE
A free nanny?

                    SLEEPING BEAUTY
A free...

Sleeping Beauty sways on her feet, eyes closed, and snores.
As she topples sideways Felicity catches her, and she wakes.

SONG 7: HAPPILY NEVER AFTER

CINDERELLA:

When traveling by pumpkin,

your dress smells like a squash.

And no one likes a twelve o'clock curfew.

Who needs glass slippers, give me Jimmy Choo.

Prince Charming leaves his stockings on the ground,

and never puts the toilet seat back down.

That wavy head of hair? Guess what, it's a toupee!

I'll take happily never after any day.

SNOW WHITE:

They're whiny. They're cranky.

They're always underfoot.

They leave a trail of carnage through the house.

I'm not talkin' seven dwarfs, just one grown spouse.

I said "I do" but didn't know the terms

meant diaper rash and rhinovirus germs.

I wanted true love's kiss; I wound up with child's play.

I'll take happily never after any day.

SLEEPING BEAUTY:

I needed some coffee,

a clock with an alarm.

I got a guy to wake me up instead,

a guy who snores all night when we're in bed.

He doesn't see I need a good night's rest.

Some NyQuil or some Ambien works best.

Give me beauty sleep, not fancy lingerie.

I'll take happily never after any day!

ALL:

Thought a prince would save me,

set me on a throne.

No one ever told me

that I could do it alone!

The fairy tale's over.

It's never what you'd think.

I spend a lot of time wondering why

a girl needs to be rescued by some guy.

I wish I knew back then what I know now.

Each princess ought to take a solemn vow.

Before some royal pain becomes your fiancé,

take happily never after any day.

Happily never after any day!

SCENE 8: The Enchanted Forest

DURING SCENE CHANGE:

> NEWSBOY
> Breaking news! Two water carriers
> hospitalized in critical condition
> after a fall at local well!

Two TREES are standing there.

> TREE 1
> You wanna go swimming?

> TREE 2
> Nah. I've only got one pair of trunks.
> (beat)
> How about a game of checkers instead?

                    TREE 1

No thanks. I'm a chestnut.

                    TREE 2

Shhhh. I think I hear someone coming.

Luna enters in her boy's costume. She pulls off her cap and
shakes her long hair free. Then she peeks into her bag, and
the light of the moon starts to glow.

                    LUNA

I don't know how long I can keep up
this disguise.

                    TREE 1

Might help to put your hat back on.

                    LUNA

    (gasps)
Did you...did you just talk?

                    TREE 2

    (gasps)
Holy cow!! A talking tree!

                    LUNA

Trees don't talk.

                    TREE 1

And moons don't run around pretending
to be human.

                    TREE 2

Relax. Your secret's safe with us.
Our bite is much worse than our bark.

                    TREE 1

Hey, if you tell a joke in a forest
and no one laughs, is it still a joke?

                    LUNA

I think I hear footsteps.

She hides behind one of the trees as Prince Jack enters.

                    PRINCE JACK
          Felicity must think I'm an idiot.

                    TREE 1
          Can you blame her?

                    LUNA
          SHHH! He'll hear you!

Jack listens, frowning. The trees fall silent and stop moving.

                    PRINCE JACK
          Great. Now I'm not just losing the
          girl -- I'm losing my mind. At this
          rate, I'll never get married.

                    LUNA
          That's not true!

Shocked, she covers her mouth with her hand.

                    PRINCE JACK
          Is someone there?

The trees try to push Luna forward. She resists, but they're
stronger and she tumbles backward -- into the prince's arms.

                    PRINCE JACK (CONT'D)
          You!? Why, hello.

                    LUNA
               (smitten)
          Hi...

                    PRINCE JACK
          We must stop bumping into each other.

                    LUNA
          I'm...sorry.

                    PRINCE JACK
          Not your fault. It's not like the
          trees pushed you, right?

Behind them, the trees high-five.

                    PRINCE JACK (CONT'D)
          Here, let me take your sack. It
          looks awfully heavy.

                    LUNA
          No!! I mean, no, thank you. I'm
          stronger than I look.

                    PRINCE JACK
          I remember being a boy your age, and
          saying that very same thing. What's
          your name?

                    LUNA
          Lu...Leo.

                    PRINCE JACK
          Leo! It's a pleasure to meet you.

                    LUNA
          I couldn't help but hear you saying
          that you were...unlucky in love.

                    PRINCE JACK
          Yeah, well, that's true.

                    LUNA
          I could help you.

                    PRINCE JACK
          You? You're just a kid!

                    LUNA
          But...I'm a very good listener.

SONG 8: PERFECT COUPLE

JACK:

When you think of history,

there are certain names you link,

loves that last forever,

couples who stayed in sync.

JFK and Jackie,

Superman and Lois Lane,

Lancelot and Guinevere,

and Tarzan and Jane.

CHORUS:

A couple of kisses,

a couple of dates,

a couple of whispers,

a couple soul mates.

If only I knew how to make her agree

how perfect a couple we'd be.

George Burns and his Gracie,

Romeo and Juliet,

Hepburn and her Tracy,

Scarlett, she fell for Rhett.

Lady and the Tramp,

Humphrey Bogart and Bacall.

Where would Ricky Ricardo be

without Lucille Ball?

CHORUS:

A couple of kisses,

a couple of dates,

a couple of whispers,

a couple soul mates.

If only I knew how to make her agree

how perfect a couple we'd be.

>   PRINCE JACK
>   If I could get her to listen to me,
>   I'd say this one thing: We could be
>   Mark Antony and Cleopatra, but without
>   the part at the end where everyone dies.
>   Or Barbie and Ken, but with a healthier
>   body image. Or Donald and Daisy, except
>   I'd be wearing pants.
>   (frustrated)
>   Oh, well, you know what I mean, right?
>   I love you!

Mickey without Minnie

is just wrong, to say the least.

What's Bert without Ernie,

Beauty without the Beast?

Siegfried needs his Roy.

Who is Bonnie without Clyde?

Where would Homer Simpson be

if Marge were not his bride?

CHORUS:

A couple of kisses,

a couple of dates,

a couple of whispers,

a couple soul mates.

If only I knew how to make her agree

that we could go down in history.

Wish there's a way I could get her to see

how perfect a couple we'd be.

When he finishes, Luna gazes at him with unbridled adoration.

                    PRINCE JACK
          Gosh, Leo. I wish I could talk to
          Felicity as easily as I talk to you.

                    TREE 1
          Well, here's your chance.

Felicity enters holding a chain saw. The trees freak out.

                    TREE 2
          She's got a chain saw! We need to
          blend in!

                         TREE 1
          Quick! Look like a tree!

                        FELICITY
               (to someone offstage)
          Glad I could help you get that pie
          off your hand, Mr. Horner! And don't
          worry -- I'm sure the doctors will be
          able to reattach your thumb!

                       PRINCE JACK
          It's Felicity. I'm gonna do it.
          I'm gonna talk to her. I'm gonna...
               (beat)
          ...Be sick.

He runs behind a tree. Felicity sees Luna and her jaw drops.

                        FELICITY
               (smitten)
          I don't think I've seen you around
          here before.

                         LUNA
          Is that...a chain saw?

                        FELICITY
          Uh, I'm not actually holding a power
          tool. Ladies would never do that. I
          was just...shaving my legs.
               (beat)
          I'm Felicity.

                         LUNA
          I'm Lu...Leo.

                        FELICITY
          Luleo. That's a beautiful name!

Jack gathers courage to emerge.

PRINCE JACK
Hello, Lady Felicity. How beest thou
on this summer day, with thy eyes
sparkling like brackish moat water?

FELICITY
Perfect timing, Jack.
    (to audience)
Just when I finally met someone
interesting!

PRINCE JACK
    (to audience)
No matter what I say to her, the
words come out like mush.

LUNA
    (to audience)
If I tell him how I really feel,
will he even notice?

SONG 9: THE WORDS I CAN'T SAY

JACK:

If I had a thousand words, it wouldn't be enough to tell you

all the ways I wish you could be mine forevermore, and, well, you

understand we could be grand. You're perfect, and I only wish you'd

see my eyes and realize how long I've waited now to kiss you.

LUNA:

If I could speak my heart, I'd tell you that you're part of me,

A piece I didn't even know till now was lost.

If you would only hear how much I hold you dear to me,

how much I wish that you could see me as I am.

FELICITY:

What is this feeling? Could I have been so wrong?

Is it as simple as finding the one you long for?

What if he looks up? Could he see me as I see him?

What if my love is all I can guarantee him?

REFRAIN:

Didn't believe in happy endings, didn't care.

That was before I saw my future standing there.

ALL VERSES AT ONCE,

Then REFRAIN

ALL:

Every night when I close my eyes, you're in my arms.

Every night I hope that my dreams might soon come true.

But then I wake and see there's no one here with me.

Every day, anyway, I will keep on waiting here for you.

> TREE 2
> That was awfully romantic.

> TREE 1
> You are such a sap!
> (to Jack)
> Go on. Ask her out.

> PRINCE JACK
> I can't ever find the words.

                    TREE 2
Well, who said you need to talk?
Throw a ball!

                    PRINCE JACK
My pitching arm's a little weak...

                    LUNA
No, Jack! This is perfect.
         (to Felicity)
Felicity, will you come to a royal
ball tomorrow night?

                    FELICITY
         (looking at Luna)
Will YOU be going?

                    LUNA
         (looking at Jack)
I wouldn't miss it for the world.

                    FELICITY
I'll see you there.
         (picks up chain saw)
Well, I should return this to someone
big and burly who would own one of
these, since it certainly doesn't
belong to delicate little me...

She exits.

                    PRINCE JACK
A ball? You're brilliant, Leo!

Luna's bag glows.

                    PRINCE JACK (CONT'D)
I can propose to Felicity there!

The glow dims. They exit.

                              TREE 1
            I think the ball was OUR idea.

                              TREE 2
            We don't get no respect.

                              TREE 1
            Hmmm. Now that they're gone, what
            should we do? I'm bored...

                              TREE 2
            Nah, I'm pretty sure you're still a
            tree.

Lights fade. They exit.

SCENE 9: Ferocia's castle

DURING SCENE CHANGE:

                             NEWSBOY
            Extra! Extra! Farmer's wife goes
            postal on three rodents with
            disabilities...

Pinocchio is serving breakfast. Gertrude stares at a carton
of orange juice on the breakfast table as Eunice watches.

                             EUNICE
            You've been staring at that carton
            of orange juice for half an hour.
            What's the problem?

                            GERTRUDE
            Shhhh! It says CONCENTRATE!

                             EUNICE
                (to Pinocchio)
            Pinocchio, I'll have the eggs.

                            PINOCCHIO
            With pleasure.

EUNICE
No, with bacon.

Ferocia is opening her mail at the breakfast table.

FEROCIA
(sips coffee and spits)
Pinocchio, this coffee tastes like
dirt!

PINOCCHIO
What do you expect!? It was ground
just this morning...

Ferocia glares at him and reads a letter.

FEROCIA
Dear Majesty, You are the perfect
ruler. Love, A Fan.
(sighs happily)
Dear Queen Ferocia, You're pretty.
(beat)
You know, Pinocchio, these letters
would be much more effective if you
made an effort to change your
handwriting.
(reads another letter)
Wait a second -- this one wasn't
written by you.

PINOCCHIO
It's from Jack and Jill. They feel
their property is too steep to be
safe and would like to trade it for
another plot of land.

FEROCIA
The ingrates. Give them [name of
rival town or school].

Prince Jack and Luna enter.

                         FEROCIA (CONT'D)
                    Did I miss something? Is this bring-an-
                    urchin-to-work day? Honestly,
                    Jack, your little...sidekick...can
                    wait outside with all the other
                    minions waiting to brighten their
                    lives with a glimpse of me...

                         PRINCE JACK
                    Aunt Ferocia, you'll never guess
                    what I've decided to do. I'm going
                    to throw a ball. I want everyone in
                    the kingdom invited!
                         (to Luna)
                    Come on. We've got a lot to do.

They exit.

                         FEROCIA
                    I think this is a splendid idea.

                         PINOCCHIO
                    You...you do?

                         FEROCIA
                    Of course. And Pinocchio -- you heard
                    my nephew. EVERYONE in the kingdom --
                    EVERYONE -- is to be invited.

                         PINOCCHIO
                    You mean...?

                         FEROCIA
                    EXACTLY.

SCENE 10: The bear cave

The Hairy Godmother steps onto the side of the stage;
Pinocchio walks in circles as the scenery gets changed.

                         HAIRY GODMOTHER
                    So the little wooden puppet --

                    PINOCCHIO
          I'm a real BOY!

                    HAIRY GODMOTHER
          Yeah, whatever -- marched bravely
          through the Enchanted Forest to the
          lair of the three bears, and
          their overgrown houseguest...

Pinocchio knocks on the door, and Mama Bear answers it.

                    MAMA BEAR
          You're too early.

She slams the door; Papa Bear answers it.

                    PAPA BEAR
          You're too late.

Slams door; Baby Bear opens it.

                    BABY BEAR
               (flirting)
          I think you're JUUUUUUST on time.

                    PINOCCHIO
          Yeah? You wanna go see a movie this
          weekend? No strings attached...

Jean-Claude pushes Baby Bear out of the way.

                    JEAN-CLAUDE
          Can I help you?

                    PINOCCHIO
          I'm here to speak to --

He breaks off as the giant appears.

                    HUGO
          What do YOU want?

PINOCCHIO

I...I...um...

He shoves the invitation at Jean-Claude and runs away.

JEAN-CLAUDE

Ouch! He gave me a splinter!
        (reading)
We've been invited to a ball.

HUGO

Very funny. What does it really
say?

JEAN-CLAUDE

See for yourself.

HUGO

    (reading the paper)
It's a trap.

BABY BEAR

Mama, can we go? Do you think that
cute puppet who was just here will
be at the ball too?

PINOCCHIO (O.S.)

I'M A REAL BOY!

JEAN-CLAUDE

Hang on a second. If everyone in
the kingdom is going to be there,
then everyone in the kingdom will
have the chance to see that you're
civilized -- not a terrifying, hideous
beast. And who knows? Maybe there's
a *jolie fille* looking for a man who
can reach the highest kitchen shelf!

HUGO

I'm not going.

                         JEAN-CLAUDE
              But master, you --

                            HUGO
              Leave me be. All of you!

He runs away.

SCENE 11: Town of Hanoveria

DURING SCENE CHANGE:

                          NEWSBOY
                 Royal ball tonight! Tickets going
                 fast!

SONG 10: ROYAL BALL

ALL:

Fasten your finest diamonds, iron your gown.

We're getting ready for a night on the town.

Dancing and singing in that big royal hall.

We're gonna have a ball!

Wonder if they'll serve a meal for lunch.

Wonder if they'll spike the cranberry punch.

Wonder if I'll get to dance with the queen.

Can't wait to see and to be seen!

Fasten your finest diamonds, iron your gown.

We're getting ready for a night on the town.

Dancing and singing in that big royal hall.

We're gonna have a ball!

Wonder if all of the bathtubs are gold.

Wouldn't that be quite a sight to behold?

Wonder if I'll cut the rug with the prince.

Can't wait to drop a couple hints!

DANCE BREAK

...The style!...The smile!

...The face!...Your Grace!

...The dress!...Success!

I've always thought I'd make great royalty,

grafted right onto that family tree.

A turn on the dance floor, a few fancy spins;

this could be how it all begins!

Fasten your finest diamonds, iron your gown.

We're getting ready for a night on the town.

Dancing and singing in that big royal hall.

We're gonna have a ball!

We're gonna have a ball!

SCENE 12: The Enchanted Forest. There is a sign that says

CASTLE (one way) and SCARY PLACE (other way).

HUMPTY DUMPTY sits on a wall, wearing a Harley-Davidson
jacket. Felicity enters.

                    FELICITY
          The ball started an hour ago...but
          I'm lost. If only I could find
          someone who could point me in the
          right direction...
               (spies Humpty)
          Oh no! Don't jump!

                  HUMPTY DUMPTY
          What's life without a thrill, man?!
          That's why I've been coasting the
          coast on my Harley -- without a
          helmet. Live free or die, man!

                    FELICITY
          Could you direct me to the castle?

                  HUMPTY DUMPTY
          I think it's that way.
               (points)
          Unless it's that way.
               (points)
          Sorry -- after inhaling all that
          exhaust, I'm a little bit scrambled.

                    FELICITY
          Hang on a second, aren't you Humpty
          Dumpty? Didn't you have a bad fall?

                  HUMPTY DUMPTY
          Yeah, but it was an AWESOME summer.
               (laughing)
          Sometimes I crack myself up! Whatsa
          matter? Can't you take a yolk?

He falls backward.

> HUMPTY DUMPTY (CONT'D)
> AAAAAAAHHHHHHH!

> FELICITY
> Oh no! Should I call all the king's
> horses and all the king's men?

> HUMPTY DUMPTY
> No, you dimwit! Call 911!

> FELICITY
> Help! Help!

As she's running, the SCARY MUSIC (SONG 11) starts, and trees
come out behind her, and WOLVES crawl up the aisles of the
audience.

> FELICITY (CONT'D)
> Oh no...I think I'm even more lost
> than I was when I started...

The wolves close in on her, dancing around her.
She screams and goes down beneath their fangs and claws.
Just then, Hugo arrives and throws them off Felicity. He
lifts her into his arms and carries her offstage.

ACT TWO

SCENE 1: Ferocia's castle

Full cast mills about at the ball.
Sleeping Beauty, Snow White, and Cinderella come forward.

                    SNOW WHITE
          I cannot believe I finally get a
          night out of the house and I have
          to bring the kids with me. Which
          reminds me -- have you seen Grumpy
          and Sneezy?

On the other side of stage, Grumpy and Sneezy stand by the punch
bowl and giggle as they drop in a frog.

                    EUNICE
            (shrieks)
          Ewww! What's that frog doing in the
          punch bowl!?

                    GRUMPY & SNEEZY
          The backstroke!

                    SNOW WHITE
          Grumpy...Sneezy! I told you...no
          pets allowed out of the cottage!

She hurries off, grabs her children's hands, and moves away.

                    SLEEPING BEAUTY
          So, now that we're here, what do you
          want to do first?

                    CINDERELLA
            (looking around)
          The bathrooms. Then the dusting,
          and I'll finish up with the vacuuming.

Luna and Prince Jack enter.

                PRINCE JACK
    Leo, why isn't Felicity here yet?

As Jack searches for Felicity, Li'l Red From The Hood approaches.

         LI'L RED FROM THE HOOD
    Yo...like the grills. You go to
    [name of local orthodontist] too?
        (beat)
    I'm Li'l Red From The Hood. Word.

                PRINCE JACK
    Um, hello.

         LI'L RED FROM THE HOOD
    Fo' shizzle.

GOLDILOCKS approaches.

              GOLDILOCKS
    Beat it, Red.

         LI'L RED FROM THE HOOD
      (to Jack)
    Facebook me, homey...

              GOLDILOCKS
    Hi, Jack. Remember me? You caught
    me breaking into the castle once?

                PRINCE JACK
    Goldilocks?

              GOLDILOCKS
    I knew you wouldn't be able to forget.

         LI'L RED FROM THE HOOD
    That's because you're on all those
    WANTED posters, fool.

                    GOLDILOCKS
        FYI, it's a misdemeanor!

The OLD WOMAN WHO LIVES IN A SHOE approaches.

            OLD WOMAN WHO LIVES IN A SHOE
        Look, sonny, I'm gonna give it to
        you straight. In this economy, I
        had to downsize to a flip-flop. I may
        not be as young as these two, but I
        get a senior discount at [name of
        local movie theater]!

                    PRINCE JACK
        Ladies...excuse me...

A commotion, as Pinocchio runs in carrying a bloody cloak.

                PRINCE JACK (CONT'D)
        That's Felicity's!

                    PINOCCHIO
        I found it in the Enchanted Forest.

                    FEROCIA
        The only beast capable of that kind
        of destruction is the giant.

Everyone gasps.

                    LUNA
        I'm sorry, Prince Jack.

                    PRINCE JACK
        I don't believe it.
            (beat)
        Don't you see, Leo? This is all
        part of the fairy tale. The middle
        bit, where the hero is tested before
        he gets the girl! We'll hunt down
        the giant and find her!

SONG 12: THE HUNT SONG

GROUP 1:

Grab a pitchfork. Grab a rake.

Grab whatever you can take.

Time to fight, for heaven's sake,

tonight.

We are standing side by side.

Cannot be preoccupied.

We will not be terrified

tonight.

No time to misunderstand,

offer up a reprimand.

He has blood upon his hand

tonight.

It will take us all to make a giant fall.

GROUP 2:

We will hunt the giant.

We will hunt the giant.

We have heard the wake-up call.

It's long past the time

to make him fall.

JACK & LUNA:

Now at last a golden opportunity

to show the one I love how much s/he means to me.

I will not stop until s/he sees

That I love him/her above all.

COMBINED

COMBINED FASTER

At the end, everyone leaves but Ferocia and Pinocchio.

> FEROCIA
> Well, that's a stroke of luck.
> Pinocchio, come along. It's my
> favorite time of the day -- when I
> walk through the [name of local
> business] parking lot and tow away
> the cars of people who aren't inside
> shopping.

As they exit, Ferocia smacks into the Hairy Godmother.

> FEROCIA (CONT'D)
> Pinocchio, make a note -- the kingdom
> needs bigger bug zappers.

> HAIRY GODMOTHER
> I'm not a mosquito. I'm a hairy
> godmother.

> PINOCCHIO
> Don't you mean a FAIR-

> HAIRY GODMOTHER
> It's a TYPO!

They shrug and exit.

HAIRY GODMOTHER (CONT'D)
Meanwhile, in a cave far, far away...

SCENE 2: The bear cave

The three bears, Jean-Claude, and Hugo stare at Felicity,
who's fast asleep.

MAMA BEAR
Someone's been sleeping in my bed.

PAPA BEAR
Someone's been sleeping in MY bed.

BABY BEAR
Someone's been --

JEAN-CLAUDE
Oui, we have all heard it before.
There's an unconscious girl on your
pillow. Get over it.

HUGO
I should have left her in the
Enchanted Forest.

JEAN-CLAUDE
Well, maybe not. Perhaps this is a
lucky break. It is not often that a
beautiful girl comes to the cave.

Felicity STIRS and SIGHS.

JEAN-CLAUDE (CONT'D)
She is waking up! Quickly, get ready!
Remember what we practiced!

HUGO
This won't work.

FELICITY
Wh...where am I?

                    JEAN-CLAUDE
          Places, everyone!
               (beat)
          Bonjour, Mademoiselle. I am
          Jean-Claude, and we would like to
          welcome you to...our little château.
          True, it may not be Versailles, but
          it beats the [name of a run-down
          local establishment]!

SONG 13: HOME SWEET HOME

JEAN-CLAUDE:

I know that you feel scared and alone,

feel like you are on your own.

I know that you think this is the end.

My lady you are among friends.

SACRE BLEU!

JEAN-CLAUDE & THREE BEARS:

Though we know your fate is scary,

no need to be solitary.

As you see us all performing,

think of this as your housewarming.

This is our home, sweet home.

Please do feel free to roam. As it will soon be known,

Home, sweet home!

So there's cobwebs in the corner.

Please don't feel like you're a foreigner.

If the ambience is lacking,

that's no reason to start packing.

This is our home, sweet home.

Please do feel free to roam.

As it will soon be known,

Home, sweet home!

So our ceiling may be leaky,

but the furniture's antiquey.

So our front room is our back room,

but you never have to vacuum!

This is our home, sweet home.

Please do feel free to roam.

As it will soon be known,

Home, sweet home!

INSTRUMENTAL BREAK

Then Hugo enters with ukulele:

I can see it may be too late

to accept me as a roommate.

I may be a little biased,

but don't hate us till you've tried us.

This is our home, sweet home.

Please do feel free to roam.

As it will soon be known,

Home, sweet home!

ALL:

This is our home, sweet home.

Please do feel free to roam.

As it will soon be known,

Home, sweet home!

Felicity exits, screaming.

> MAMA BEAR
> But we haven't gotten to the reprise!

> JEAN-CLAUDE
> Maybe she isn't a fan of the ukulele.

> HUGO
> I TOLD YOU SO!!!!

They slink away.

> HUGO (CONT'D)
> I might as well just accept it. I'm
> a freak. Sure, I'll know it's raining
> before anyone else does...and there's
> the occasional slam dunk...but I'll
> never be the man I used to be. And
> who could fall in love with THIS?

SONG 14: IT'S LONELY AT THE TOP

HUGO:

Look, how I'm standing alone here

even when there's a crowd,

and if you listen, you can hear my heart break with

words I can't speak out loud.

Where's that someone who is long overdue,

that fine kind of love that won't stop?

Here, I've been waiting a lifetime.

It's lonely at the top.

Sure, I'm a taste that's acquired,

No fairy-tale white knight.

I need a princess who sees under the surface,

a love at second sight.

Where's that someone who will try something new?

No need to comparison shop.

Here, I've been waiting a lifetime.

It's lonely at the top.

BRIDGE

Out there is someone who will love me just for me.

Out there is a future full of possibility.

Still, for every salt there's a pepper.

Each Sonny has a Cher.

For every jelly, there's some smooth peanut butter.

The world is full of pairs.

Where's that someone who can make this one two?

A partner who I'll never swap.

Dear, I've been waiting a lifetime.

It's lonely at the top.

SCENE 3: The Enchanted Forest

DURING SCENE CHANGE:

> NEWSBOY
> Get your news here! Princess
> bruised; sues frozen pea manufacturer!

A tower, with a ladder propped up against it. THREE PIGS
wearing construction helmets are arguing over blueprints.
A WOLF stands nearby.

> PORKY
> Hey, can you get me some 2x4s?

> HAMLET
> Sure. How long do you need them?

> PORKY
> Better make it a few months. I gotta
> build a whole staircase, here.

                    FRANCIS BACON
          Well, be careful. I heard about a
          guy who lost his whole left side in
          a construction accident.
                    (beat)
          He's all right now.

Luna and Jack walk in.

                    LUNA
          Oh no! It's a swine flu quarantine
          zone!

The wolf approaches Luna and Prince Jack.

                    BLITZER
          I'm afraid you can't be here.

                    LUNA
              (to Jack)
          I told you so.

                    BLITZER
          I'm Wolf Blitzer, foreman of [name
          of local construction company], and
          this is an active work...
                    (looooong beat)
          ...Zone.

                    PRINCE JACK
          What's with the big pause?

Blitzer holds up his hands in front of him.

                    BLITZER
          I dunno. I was born with them.

Suddenly a hairbrush gets thrown down from the tower
and hits Prince Jack. RAPUNZEL, wearing a head scarf,
appears.

                    RAPUNZEL
You lazy, boneheaded good-for-nothing!
         (beat)
Oh. Sorry. You're not Sheldon.

                     LUNA
Who's Sheldon?

                    RAPUNZEL
The lazy, boneheaded good-for-nothing
who was supposed to rescue me from
this tower by moonlight. But there
was no moonlight, so what did he do?

                  PRINCE JACK
I give up.

                    RAPUNZEL
ABSOLUTELY NOTHING.

PRINCE SHELDON runs in.

                 PRINCE SHELDON
Rapunzel, Rapunzel! Let down your
long hair, my love!

                    RAPUNZEL
You're too late, Sheldon.

                 PRINCE SHELDON
I swear by the moon, Rapunzel --

                    RAPUNZEL
Fat lot of good THAT'LL do you!

                     LUNA
    (her bag glows, then fades)
Oh my gosh! No moonlight! I never
realized...

                  PRINCE JACK
I know! Girls can be so irrational!

                        LUNA

Irrational!?

                      RAPUNZEL

Irrational?!

                   PRINCE SHELDON

Why is this construction crew here?

                      RAPUNZEL

I hired them.

She takes off her scarf -- her hair is short.

                   PRINCE SHELDON
              (gasps)
You cut your beautiful hair?!

                      RAPUNZEL

Yes! I traded it to a wig maker for
cash. Turns out I don't need a prince --
just a staircase.

                   PRINCE SHELDON
              (to Jack)
Tell her she's making a big mistake.

                      RAPUNZEL
              (to Luna)
Tell him the only mistake was waiting
around for him.
              (beat)
I have two words for you, Sheldon: THE END.

                   PRINCE SHELDON

You know what? I don't need you and
your fancy salon conditioner, and
your dandruff phobia. I'm tired of
finding your hair in my sink all the
time. I just passed Little Miss
Muffet on her tuffet, and I bet she'd
be HAPPY to share her curds and whey!

He exits.

> LUNA
> (to Jack)
> You can't just let him walk off!

> PRINCE JACK
> Yes, I can! I need to find Felicity!

> LUNA
> How do you have any hope of finding
> true love if you won't help anyone
> else find it?

> PRINCE JACK
> Okay, okay.
> (to Sheldon, offstage)
> Hey, Sheldon -- by any chance, are you
> afraid of spiders?

SONG 15: DISENCHANTED

RAPUNZEL:

Call me naïve in my tall ivory tower,

waiting and waiting with each passing hour,

nothing to do as my hair slowly grew,

pining away for a guy who didn't come.

What did I get but a braid and a headache?

Which slowly spread to a wish-I-were-dead ache.

Swore to myself this was bad for my health,

that I would never again act quite so dumb.

Guess you could say I'm a bit disenchanted.

Don't wanna wait for my wish to be granted.

Time to rescue myself because I cannot believe

that fairy tales come true.

That scenic view from my room wasn't rosy,

locked in a cell that was less and less cozy.

And it got worse when I tried to converse

with bats and bugs who rarely answered back.

Stuck in a prison, a girl can go crazy.

Some of the details have gotten quite hazy.

Knew it was time for this sister to climb

down and get my future on its track.

Guess you could say I'm a bit disenchanted.

Don't wanna wait for my wish to be granted.

Time to rescue myself because I cannot believe

that fairy tales come true.

LUNA:

When it comes to love, you shoot for the stars.

When it comes to love, no journey's too far.

Love is worth waiting for.

Love conquers all

right from the moment you fall.

RAPUNZEL:

Honey, don't wait for some grand love affair.

Just wash that man right out of your hair.

Know in my heart that I have to be smart,

stop falling for a prince with just one glance.

LUNA:

You read the stories while still in your cradle.

Life without love: it can often be fatal.

Some knucklehead who's not easily led:

maybe he deserves a second chance.

BOTH:

Every word he whispers

is a secret tune.

Every one of his kisses, I know,

will send me over the moon.

Maybe I won't be disenchanted.

Change the story so it's not slanted.

I can rescue myself because I still believe

that fairy tales come true.

SCENE 4: The bear cave

DURING SCENE CHANGE:

>   NEWSBOY
>   Social Services condemns living
>   conditions of large family in a
>   shoe...Read all about it!

Jean-Claude enters with a bowl.

>   JEAN-CLAUDE
>   Ah, *bonjour*, Mademoiselle. I've
>   brought you some porridge.

>   FELICITY
>   Porridge?

>   JEAN-CLAUDE
>   *Oui.* It's not very exciting, but at
>   least it's not too hot or too cold.

Felicity takes the bowl.

>   FELICITY
>   Thank you for being so kind to me.
>   Especially when I've been so rude.

>   JEAN-CLAUDE
>   My master -- you know, he wasn't always
>   this way.

>   FELICITY
>   You mean a giant?

>   JEAN-CLAUDE
>   He prefers "vertically gifted."
>   (beat)
>   I'm just saying...underneath all
>   that...height...he's not so bad.

                    HUGO (O.S.)
I mean it, Little Boy Blue. I don't
care if you're Louis Armstrong! You
pick up that stupid horn again, and
I'm calling the cops!

He stumbles onto the stage.

                    HUGO (CONT'D)
               (sourly)
Oh, great. It's you.

                    JEAN-CLAUDE
               (stands, to Felicity)
I'm just saying.

He exits.

                    FELICITY
I...want to thank you. For saving
my life in the woods.

                    HUGO
If I'd known you were like the rest
of them, I would have left you there.

                    FELICITY
The rest of who?

                    HUGO
All those silly girls who only care
about looks.

                    FELICITY
You don't know anything about me!

                    HUGO
I know you can't stand to be in the
same room as me. In some cultures,
you know, I'd be considered tall,
dark, and handsome.

                    FELICITY

You're tall, all right. And when
it's dark, you're handsome.

                    HUGO

Well, at least I'm not deaf, dumb,
and BLONDE.

                    FELICITY

Can you get satellite reception up
there?

                    HUGO

Oh, I guess that last insult went
over your head...

                    FELICITY

Fee Fie Foe Fum.

They growl at each other.

SONG 16: DRIVING ME CRAZY

FELICITY:

Never felt like this before.

My blood pressure's starting to soar.

These are feelings I can't ignore.

It's true he's driving me crazy!

HUGO:

Must confess that this is a first.

Feel my head is going to burst.

And I think it's gonna get worse.

It's true she's driving me crazy!

FELICITY: He's a few puppies shy of a pet shop.

HUGO: She's several links short of a chain.

FELICITY: He's eating with a single chopstick.

HUGO: Her silo's missing all its grain.

FELICITY: The oven's on, but nothing's cooking.

HUGO: One taco's gone from her lunch plate.

FELICITY: Takes him two hours to watch 60 Minutes.

HUGO & FELICITY: It's true, it's you I hate!

FELICITY:

Maybe, you could take a long walk off a short pier.

Baby, how I wish you weren't here!

FELICITY:	HUGO:
Maybe,	Must confess that this is a first.
you could take a long	Feel my head is going to burst.
walk off a short pier.	
Baby,	And I think it's gonna get worse.
It's true you're driving	It's true you're driving
me crazy!	me crazy!

FELICITY: I think the cheese slid off his cracker.

HUGO: She'd move to Phoenix and build an igloo.

FELICITY: He fell out of his family tree.

HUGO: Is that your shoe size or IQ?

FELICITY: He's several feet short of the runway.

HUGO: She's fishing but she's missing bait.

FELICITY: He's just a few clowns shy of a circus.

HUGO & FELICITY:

It's true, it's you I hate!

Never felt like this before,

but it's you I do abhor.

And I will forevermore.

It's true you're driving me crazy.

It's true you're driving me crazy!

SCENE 5: The Enchanted Forest

DURING SCENE CHANGE:

NEWSBOY
Extra! Extra! Giant beanstalk prompts
organic farmers to protest in front of
[name of local grocery store]!

The trees are standing at attention.

TREE 2
Did you hear about the snare drum
and the cymbals that fell out of the
tree?

DRUM: Badummmm TSSSSSH.
Luna and Prince Jack enter.

PRINCE JACK

Prince Sheldon and Rapunzel agreed
to do couples counseling with Mother
Goose. She's good. She got Jack Be
Nimble to kick his pyromania habit.

LUNA

I hope it works out for them. There's
nothing like true love.

PRINCE JACK

I guess you'd know. A guy as romantic
as you must have a girlfriend.

LUNA

Oh, um...well...

PRINCE JACK

What's she like?

LUNA

Well, uh, she's...
        (looks at Jack)
About this tall.
        (measures Jack's
        height. As she talks,
        her light starts
        glowing)
She's got dark hair...and brown eyes
you could drown in...and big strong
arms that can bench-press an ox...

PRINCE JACK

Bench-press an ox?

LUNA

        (flustered, light
        fading)
Um...she's the women's wrestling
champ in my village.

                    PRINCE JACK
          She sounds great.
               (beat)
          Want me to carry your bag for a while?
          We've been walking for a long time.

                    LUNA
          Oh! No, thanks, I've got it.

                    PRINCE JACK
          What's in there, anyway?

                    LUNA
          Just a few essentials. Toothpaste.
          Tylenol. Whoopie cushion.

                    PRINCE JACK
          You're hiding something. Let me see.

He reaches for the sack but Luna wrenches it away as it
glows for a moment. Jack reels backward, bumping into THREE
BLIND MICE wearing sunglasses who've stumbled onto the stage.

                    MICKEY
          Hey! Watch where you're going.

                    PRINCE JACK
          I beg your pardon!
               (beat)
          Can you help me? I'm looking for a
          beautiful lady, who may have been
          attacked by a giant in these woods.

                    MINNIE
          Have you seen her lately?

                    PRINCE JACK
          No.

                    ALGERNON
          Neither have we!!

They all laugh.

                    LUNA
         You must be the three blind mice.

                  ALGERNON
         Hickory Dickory Dock, the mouse ran
         up the clock...the clock struck one,
         but the rest of us got away with
         minor eye injuries.

                   MICKEY
         We're the three visually challenged
         mice, if you don't mind.

                  ALGERNON
         I prefer "optically darker."

                   MINNIE
         Or "photonically non-receptive."

                 PRINCE JACK
         Frankly, I think this political
         correctness has gotten out of hand.

SONG 17: THE PC SONG

MICKEY, MINNIE & ALGERNON:

INTRO:

The world has changed -- these days

you might find yourself in trouble

to call a spade a spade,

when it would rather be a shovel.

I don't know how it happened, but frankly I suspect

we've gone too far to make ourselves politically correct.

Red Riding Hood's the one to blame for her incessant whining.

The Big Bad Wolf was simply fond of inter-species dining.

"What big teeth you have," Red said, according to the fable.

Should have said the wolf was orthodontically able.

Come across three little pigs that you would like to greet.

Refer to them instead as the Other White Meat.

Mother Hubbard now is chronologically gifted.

Seven dwarfs insist they're only vertically unlifted.

A hurricane's a himmacane.

A heroine's a hero.

A name can be a judgment call,

so make sure that you're clear, oh.

It's always hard to find a word

on which we all agree.

Don't offend 'cause that's the trend,

Or else we're not PC.

Now we know that Cinderella just misunderstood.

The evil stepmother has potential to be good.

She's not the only villain who's been unfairly cursed.

Those ugly stepsisters were cosmetically diverse.

Jack Sprat's wife was never fat, just differently weighted.

Sleeping Beauty's certain she was medically sedated.

Amphibian American's the new term for Frog Prince.

And Goldilocks, she's not a blonde, her hair just sometimes glints.

A hurricane's a himmacane.

A heroine's a hero.

A name can be a judgment call,

so make sure that you're clear, oh.

It's always hard to find a word

on which we all agree.

Don't offend 'cause that's the trend,

or else we're not PC.

(SLOW):

No one ever argues, instead we all can share.

No one's ever bald, they're follically impaired...

If you want to tell yourself we live in harmony,

don't offend, 'cause that's the trend.

Make yourself PC.

Make yourself PC.

> MICKEY
> We haven't seen that girl of yours,
> but we'll keep an eye out.

ALGERNON
Metaphorically speaking, of course.

MINNIE
Hey, kid, what's in the bag?

Luna's light glows, and fades.

LUNA
Come on, Jack. We better keep going.

They exit -- and the mice whip off their sunglasses and take
out walkie-talkies.

MINNIE
This is Special Agent Cheddar. Do
you read me, Pussycat?

Pinocchio and Ferocia appear on the side of the stage.

PINOCCHIO
Your majesty, it's the secure line.

His nose grows, and he takes out a second phone from his
pocket and listens in.

FEROCIA
Pussycat here. What have you got
for me, Agent Cheddar?

MINNIE
The prince is on the move. I repeat,
on the move. The Mousetrap has failed.

They exit.

FEROCIA
(hanging up)
Pinocchio, this calls for a disguise.
I need to look like an old hag.
(holds up her palm)
DON'T say it.

Pinocchio helps her dress as an old hag.

> FEROCIA (CONT'D)
> All I have to do is offer him
> something completely irresistible...
> a magical parking pass.
> > (She brandishes it)
> One which just also happens to be
> poisoned.

Luna and Jack reappear. On the side of the stage, Hairy Godmother enters and starts doing her nails.

> TREE 1
> I don't feel good about this.

> TREE 2
> Me neither. I'm petrified.

> LUNA
> Maybe we should go back...

> PRINCE JACK
> We can't. Felicity is still out
> there.

An old woman appears (Ferocia), carrying a huge bag.

> FEROCIA
> Oh, my. I'm an old woman who's weary
> and needs a moment of rest and who
> looks nothing at all like your
> auntie.

> PRINCE JACK
> Why, let me help you.

He takes her arm. Luna pulls him away.

> LUNA
> Your highness, I don't trust her.

                         PRINCE JACK
          Leo, don't be paranoid! This nice
          lady probably lost her way!

                          FEROCIA
          Oh, that's right. I know I have a
          bus schedule somewhere.
                    (rummages through bag
                    and pulls out pass)
          Why, look at what I found. A parking
          pass for a magical spot that appears
          anytime you need it on Main Street!

Prince Jack's head snaps forward. He is bewitched.

                         PRINCE JACK
          Me likeeeeee...

                           LUNA
          Don't fall for it, Jack!

                          FEROCIA
          Even at noontime!

As Jack snatches it out of Ferocia's hand, Luna cries out.
Ferocia runs off as Jack begins to contort and groan.

                         PRINCE JACK
          It's...EXPIRED!!!!!!!!!!!!!

He dies.

                           LUNA

          JAAAAAAAAAACK!!!

                       HAIRY GODMOTHER
                    (sighs)
          I haven't even finished my top coat.
                    (dutifully)
          Meanwhile, back at the bear cave...

                    LUNA
          Hang on a second, you can't just
          leave him dead like this.

The three mice stumble in across the stage.

                  ALGERNON
          We don't use the term "dead" anymore.

                   MICKEY
          It's "metabolically challenged."

                   MINNIE
          Or "living impaired."

They stumble offstage.

               HAIRY GODMOTHER
          Honey, I'm in the business of midnight
          formalwear, not miracles. Although
          Cinderella came close. You should
          have seen her before I got hold of
          a pair of tweezers and a girdle...

Cinderella enters.

                 CINDERELLA
             (angry)
          Hey, you oversized moth: You. Me.
          Behind the carriage shed. Right now.

               HAIRY GODMOTHER
          Kinda busy here...

                 CINDERELLA
          And for the record, I do not have and
          never did have a unibrow!

Makes a sassy gesture and flounces off.

                    LUNA
          Can't you wave your wand or something?

                    HAIRY GODMOTHER
          Nope. His insurance won't cover it.

                         LUNA
          We have to do something!

They pick up Jack's arms and legs and drag him offstage.

                        TREE 1
          Wait a second...the mice weren't
          really blind? And Ferocia wants to
          kill her own nephew? And Cinderella
          had a unibrow?

                        TREE 2
          Beats me. I'm stumped.

SCENE 6: The bear cave garden

DURING SCENE CHANGE:

                       NEWSBOY
          Lost sheep found alive but dehydrated
          after surviving subzero temperatures
          overnight! Little Bo Peep overjoyed!

Mama Bear and Felicity weed. Felicity pulls out a whole plant.

                      MAMA BEAR
          Dear, the weeds are the things WITHOUT
          the flowers.

                       FELICITY
          Oh...sorry.

Hugo and Jean-Claude enter and watch the ladies.

                     JEAN-CLAUDE
          It's just a little small talk.

                        HUGO
          No wonder I stink at it.

                    JEAN-CLAUDE
          Bonjour, how are you today?

                       HUGO
          Fine, thanks.

                    JEAN-CLAUDE
          Not you. Felicity.

                       HUGO
          Well, how would I know? I'm not
          speaking to her!

Jean-Claude SIGHS.

                    JEAN-CLAUDE
          Mama Bear, can you help me in the
          kitchen?

He pantomimes getting the other two together, and she nods
and follows. Hugo sits and yanks a plant out by its neck.

                      FELICITY
          You're only supposed to pick the
          little green things on the ends.

                       HUGO
          I hate beanstalks.

                      FELICITY
          Come to think of it, I hate broccoli.

She picks the broccoli and hurls it offstage. Hugo grins.

                       HUGO
          Wow! You've got a great arm!

                      FELICITY
          Well, um, it's not like I practice
          my pitching or anything. That
          wouldn't be very ladylike.

                         HUGO
          Then you should steer clear of these
          hot peppers. A lady's constitution
          is too delicate to handle them.

He eats one.

                         FELICITY
          Oh, REALLY?

She eats two -- and then lets out an enormous burp. Hugo
looks at her and burps even longer. Hugo grabs a watermelon,
takes a bite, and spits a seed. He hands her a wedge of
melon, and she does the same -- and spits it farther.

                         HUGO
               (laughing)
          You're incredible!

                         FELICITY
          Yeah. I make a great guy. And a
          really lousy lady.

                         HUGO
          Who cares?

                         FELICITY
          Everyone, that's who. I'm supposed
          to laugh daintily and rock a tiara
          and dance waltzes -- when I'd rather
          be fishing or hiking or skydiving.

                         HUGO
          Skydiving!?

                         FELICITY
          What? Are you afraid of heights?

                         HUGO
          You gotta be kidding me.

                    FELICITY
     I have to work so hard to be someone
     I'm not...it's exhausting. Nobody
     ever sees the real me.

                    HUGO
          (softly)
     I know what you mean.
          (beat)
     I don't know much about wearing
     tiaras, but I can teach you to dance.

                    FELICITY
     You don't want to do that. At my
     last ball, I broke all eleven of my
     dance partner's toes.

                    HUGO
     Believe me -- I won't feel a thing.

SONG 18: DRIVING ME CRAZY (Reprise)

FELICITY:

Never felt like this before.

My blood pressure's starting to soar.

These are feelings I can't ignore.

It's true you're driving me crazy.

HUGO:

Must confess that this is a first.

Feel my head is going to burst.

And I think it's gonna get worse.

It's true you're driving me crazy.

(MUSICAL INTERLUDE)

BOTH:

Never felt like this before,

but it's you I do adore,

and I will forevermore.

It's true you're driving me crazy.

It's true you're driving me crazy.

SCENE 7: Ferocia's castle

DURING SCENE CHANGE:

>   NEWSBOY
> Extra! Extra! Thanks to [Insert
> name of local shelter], elderly
> housewife and pet dog no longer face
> starvation!

Ferocia is pacing when Pinocchio enters with the three mice.
Eunice and Gertrude are reading by candlelight.

>   PINOCCHIO
> It's done, your majesty.

>   FEROCIA
> You're sure?

>   MINNIE
> We saw it with our own eyes.

>   MICKEY
> In a matter of speaking, anyway.

>   ALGERNON
> It's as clear as the braille on the
> wall: Jack is biologically defunct.

                    PINOCCHIO
Huh?

                     MINNIE
It's the politically correct term
for "dead."

                    FEROCIA
Excellent. And the girl?

                     MICKEY
Not quite as dead. The giant has
her at the bears' cave.

                    FEROCIA
You three know what must be done...?

The mice salute and exit.

                     EUNICE
       (gasps)
Mama, Jack's dead?

                    GERTRUDE
But that's AWFUL!

                    FEROCIA
Of course it is, darlings. We're
heartbroken, aren't we, Pinocchio?

                    PINOCCHIO
Oh yes.

His nose grows.

                    FEROCIA
It's perfectly normal to grieve.
       (beat, then briskly)
All right, time to move on with our
lives...come along, Pinocchio.

They exit, leave the girls alone.

                              EUNICE
          Why would Mama want Jack dead?

                              GERTRUDE
          I don't get it.

                              EUNICE
          There's lots about Mama I don't
          understand.

SONG 19: IF MAMA WERE NORMAL

GERTRUDE & EUNICE:

Some kids never travel by broom.

They have a station wagon.

Some kids get a puppy to love,

not a fiery dragon.

They've got a playroom to hold all their toys

instead of a dungeon that's cold.

Wouldn't that be quite a sight to behold

if only

Mama were normal.

GERTRUDE:

I bring a boy home and constantly fear

he'll get turned into a toad.

EUNICE:

Sometimes it seems that my whole life

is a Buffy episode.

BOTH:

When baking cookies, you don't have to add

poison right into the mix.

What will come next from her bag of tricks?

If only

Mama were normal.

BRIDGE

To get an allowance, we have to tuck

each flying monkey in bed.

June Cleaver, please,

We're down on our knees,

could you adopt us instead!?

Some kids vacation to beaches with sun,

Not Guantanamo Bay.

Some kids never learn magical spells.

Instead they take ballet.

Some parents don't set the school roof on fire

during the class show-and-tell.

I really think it would be pretty swell

if only

Mama were normal.

If only

>   FEROCIA
> Girls, have you finished cleaning the
> torture chamber?

>   GIRLS
> Yes, Mama.

Mama were normal.

>   EUNICE (CONT'D)
> We might be too late to save Jack --
> but we're not too late to save Felicity.

>   GERTRUDE
> We don't know where the giant lives.

Pinocchio walks in.

>   EUNICE
> But he does.

>   GERTRUDE
> Pinocchio, you know where Felicity
> is. We heard you.

>   PINOCCHIO
> Gee, look at the time...

>   EUNICE
> If you don't spill, Pinocchio, you
> won't just NEED crutches...you'll BE
> crutches.

>   PINOCCHIO
> You sure are your mother's daughters.
>   (beat)
> This way...

SCENE 8: A meadow with cottage

DURING SCENE CHANGE:

> NEWSBOY
> Country home vandalized! Blonde
> arrested for breaking and entering!

Goldilocks rushes across stage, laughing maniacally and brandishing stolen loot.

The Hairy Godmother and Luna drag Prince Jack's body in front of Cinderella's cottage.

> HAIRY GODMOTHER
> Good luck, sister!

Luna knocks on the door.

> LUNA
> Hello! Hello? Can someone help me?

Sleeping Beauty opens the door.

> SLEEPING BEAUTY
> Is it naptime already?!

She curls up next to Jack's body. Cinderella comes outside holding a pumpkin. Snow White and Grumpy and Sneezy hover at the doorway.

> CINDERELLA
> He's not asleep. He's dead.

> GRUMPY & SNEEZY
> DEAD!?!

> SNOW WHITE
> (with Grumpy and Sneezy)
> Hello, there are CHILDREN present!
> (MORE)

                    SNOW WHITE (CONT'D)
They don't even know what happened
to Bambi's mother. We fast-forward.

                         LUNA
There must be something you can do!

                      CINDERELLA
Maybe Sleeping Beauty is right.

                         LUNA
What do you mean?

                      SNOW WHITE
Well, dead in a fairy tale isn't
100% dead.

                   SLEEPING BEAUTY
     (yawning)
Yeah, it's not like AIG dead.

                      SNOW WHITE
Or Bush Administration dead.

                      CINDERELLA
Or Britney-Spears's-career dead.
     (beat)
Sometimes you get a second chance.

                      SNOW WHITE
True love's kiss worked for each of
us. Why wouldn't it work for him?

                         LUNA
His true love was stolen by the giant.
How am I supposed to find her?

                      CINDERELLA
Prince Charming plays poker with the
giant's butler, Jean-Claude. I can
get you there.
                      (MORE)

                    CINDERELLA (CONT'D)
                (beat)
Not that I want to endorse the
archetypical I-need-to-be-saved-in-order-
to-get-a-happy-ending idea.

                    SLEEPING BEAUTY
But this time around, it's the prince
who needs saving!

                    SNOW WHITE
And besides -- this is always the
best part of the story. Are you
sure you want him resurrected, though?

                    SLEEPING BEAUTY
He might snore.

                    CINDERELLA
Or be a total pig.

                        LUNA
But you don't love someone because
they're perfect. You love them even
if they're not.

                    SLEEPING BEAUTY
Oh my gosh. You're right.
                (calls offstage)
Honey? Wanna go rent a Disney movie?

                    SNOW WHITE
                (calls offstage)
Sweetie? Wanna change Bashful's
diaper?

                    CINDERELLA
Baby? Wanna take a ride...
                (she lifts the top
                off the pumpkin she
                is holding)
...In the convertible?

They all start to rush offstage till Luna calls.

                         LUNA
          Could you take me to the giant's
          cave before you go out on your dates?

                      SNOW WHITE
          Oh, right.

                    SLEEPING BEAUTY
          Let's make it fast, girls.

                      CINDERELLA
          Totally. I need to be back before
          the stroke of midnight.

They exit with Jack's body.

SCENE 9: On the apron of the stage

                       FEROCIA
          Pinocchio? Pinocchio. PINOCCHIO!

Spies a note and reads it aloud.

                   FEROCIA (CONT'D)
          Dear Your Majesty, sorry I'm not
          here. I had tickets to a Jonas
          Brothers concert. Love, Pinocchio.
          PS Don't kill me.
               (beat)
          Must I do everything myself?

Grabs sword and stalks off.

SCENE 10: The bear cave

Eunice, Gertrude, and Pinocchio are in the lair.

                     JEAN-CLAUDE
          Why should we trust anyone who works
          for or is related to Ferocia?

>   GERTRUDE
>   Because we're pretty?

>   PINOCCHIO
>   What have you got to lose?

>   BABY BEAR
>   Our heads?

Suddenly the princesses arrive, with Luna and Prince Jack.

>   PAPA BEAR
>   I'm not running a funeral parlor.

>   MAMA BEAR
>   Bruno, the boy can't help being dead.

>   SNOW WHITE
>   He needs true love's kiss.

>   LUNA
>   Is Felicity here?

Felicity and Hugo enter holding hands. She sees Jack's body.

>   FELICITY
>   Jack?? Oh no.

>   LUNA
>   You have to kiss him.

>   FELICITY
>   But --

>   LUNA
>   Please.

Felicity bends down and kisses Prince Jack -- while Hugo
storms away, angry. Prince Jack sits up.

>   PRINCE JACK
>   Hmmm...nope, nothing.

He drops dead again.

                    LUNA
          What? What's wrong?

                    CINDERELLA
          Sometimes the person you think is
          your true love isn't your true love
          after all.

                    SLEEPING BEAUTY
          What she means is: kiss him.

Luna bends down and kisses Jack, who sits up, kissing her
fiercely, and then breaks off.

                    PRINCE JACK
          Leo...?!
               (manly)
          So, uh, how about those [Insert name
          of local NFL team]?

Ferocia arrives, brandishing a sword.

                    FEROCIA
               (to Jack)
          What's this? You should be dead...
               (to Hugo)
          And YOU, brother -- I am not going
          to let you ruin this for me again!

She runs at Hugo with her sword, but Felicity jumps between
the sword and Hugo to save him.

                    FELICITY
          Don't! I love him!

Suddenly, the bag Luna's been carrying starts to glow. A
transformation: her long hair falls from her hat and we see
she is the moon. At the same time, Hugo transforms from
giant to king.

PRINCE JACK
    (to Luna)
Whoa. Does this mean you're not a dude?
    (to Hugo)
And you -- you're my father?

HUGO
Yes, son. I was king of Hanoveria
until that witch put a spell on me
that could only be broken by true
love -- but who would ever love a giant?

FELICITY
Someone with a very, very big heart.

They kiss.

HUGO
Pinocchio, seize her. Ferocia, you're
going away for a long, long time. I'm
exiling you to a Dostoevsky novel. And
Jack...I think someone's waiting for you.

PRINCE JACK
    (to Luna)
Um, uhh...you're looking so lunar tonight.
Not because you're big and round, obviously,
but because you're, um, bright...

LUNA
Jack, it's still me.

PRINCE JACK
    (relieved)
Wanna grab a burger?

LUNA
I can't. Now that I know humans CAN
find true love, I have to go back.

PRINCE JACK
But I only just found you!

                         LUNA
            Well...you could come with me.

                     HAIRY GODMOTHER
            And that is how there came to be a
            man on the moon...

                     JEAN-CLAUDE
            Monsieur, I don't mean to nitpick,
            but the man ON the moon is Neil
            Armstrong. Don't you mean the man
            IN the moon?

                          ALL
            IT'S A TYPO!

SONG 20: ONCE IN A BLUE MOON

CINDERELLA/SNOW WHITE/SLEEPING BEAUTY:

Once I was a cynic,

but now I'm convinced.

I like it when the princess

can rescue the prince!

SOLOISTS (3):

Don't matter if you're tiny.

Don't matter if you're tall.

Love sends you to the moon

and makes a giant fall.

GERTRUDE & EUNICE:

And most of all, this is true.

Can't go looking for love, 'cause it will

Holy cow, stop me now!

Come and find you!

ALL:

It's gonna hit you from behind.

It's gonna sweep you off your feet.

You lose your heart and lose your mind.

That someone special that you meet

once

in a blue moon.

VERSE 1:

If you are certain you are lost and on your own,

Out there is someone else who also feels alone.

Don't settle for a lonely game of solitaire

when you can join your hands and you become a pair!

It's gonna hit you from behind.

It's gonna sweep you off your feet.

You lose your heart and lose your mind.

That someone special that you meet

once

in a blue moon.

SOLOISTS (3):

Your tongue is tied in knots.

You're dizzy and you swoon.

Your heart is beating faster,

but you're over the moon.

GIRLS:

You're only seeing him.

The rest is a blur.

BOYS:

You don't know where you're goin',

but you know it's with her!

VERSE 2:

Love is patient.

Love is kind.

Love is deaf and dumb and blind.

Love at first sight.

Love's first kiss.

Cupid's arrow doesn't miss.

VERSE 1 & 2 TOGETHER:

ALL:

It's gonna hit you from behind.

It's gonna sweep you off your feet.

You lose your heart and lose your mind.

That someone special that you meet

once

in a blue moon.

Holy cow, stop me now!

Once

once in a blue moon!

SHEET MUSIC

Over the Moon

Lyrics by
Jodi Picoult

Music by
Ellen Wilber

all   right from the mo - ment you   fall._____

LUNA:

STELLA & BELLA:

Some - day I will find __ the guy _____ of my dreams. ____   Some - day

Some - day I will find __ the guy _____ of my dreams. ____   Some - day

I will find __ a fel - la __ who seems   like he was meant for __ me,

I will find __ a fel - la __ who seems   like he was meant for __ me,

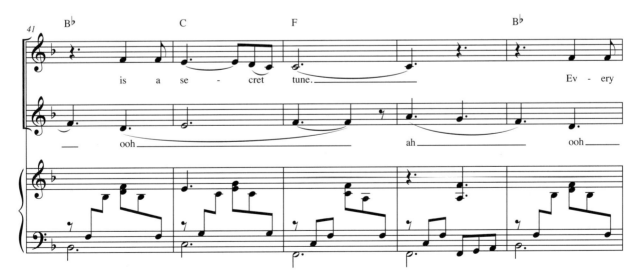

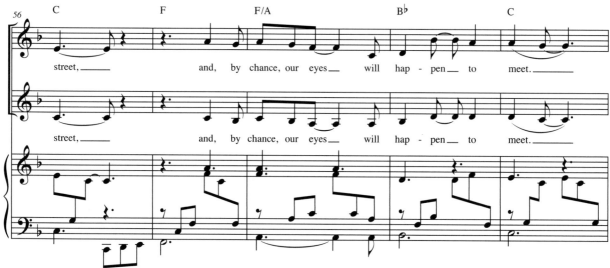

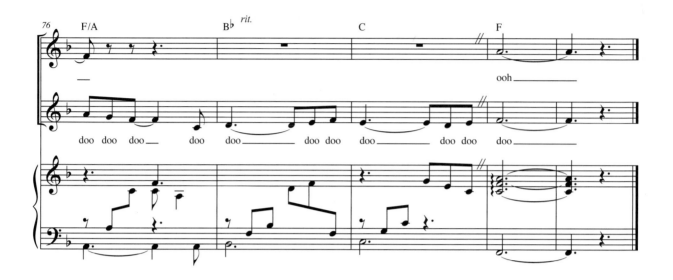

Wonderful Morning

Lyrics by
Jodi Picoult

Music by
Ellen Wilber

NEWSBOY: Good morning, Hanoveria!!!

It's a won-der-ful morn - ing. It's gon-na be_____ a won-der-ful day._____

Stop and chat with a friend,_____ or watch the world pass_____ by from a ca-fé._____

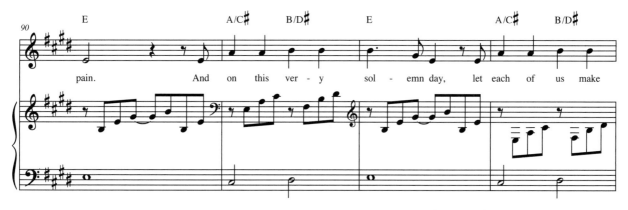

when the gi - ant came for him and tore him up from limb to limb, he

saw the fut - ure look - ing grim and in - ter - vened. He

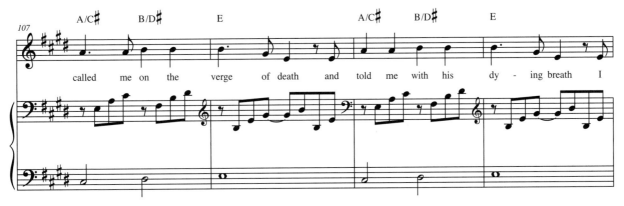

called me on the verge of death and told me with his dy - ing breath I

ALL:

must sur - vive him none - the - less. Long live the queen.

Guess it's true that life ___ can change in the blink of an eye. ___

We love liv - ing here. Can't you see why? ___

NEWSBOY:
Extra! Extra!
Gay marriage law

passes! Butcher, baker, and candlestick maker give it a thumbs-up! ALL:

U. S. News did its rank - ing. We nabbed the high -

- - est spot of them all. ___ Just one small bit of troub - le, and it is stand -

Wonderful Morning

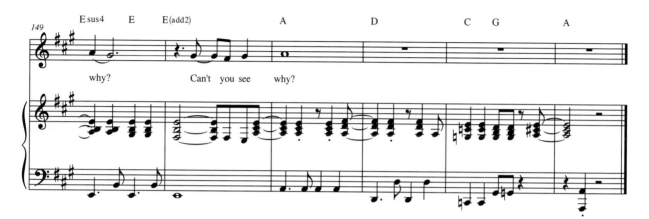

why?   Can't you see   why?

Wonderful Morning (reprise)

Lyrics by
Jodi Picoult

Music by
Ellen Wilber

ALL:
It's a won-der-ful morn - ing. It's gon-na be_____ a won-der-ful day._

Stop and chat with a friend,_____ or watch the world pass_____ by from a ca-fé._

See the beau-ti-ful scene - ery. Smell the fresh air_____ and take a deep breath._

Best town ev-er to live_____ in 'cept for the threat_____ of sud-den death!_

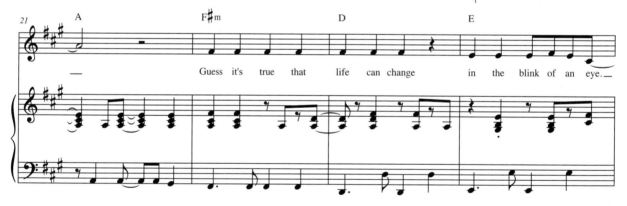

Guess it's true that life can change in the blink of an eye._

We love liv-ing here. Can't_ you see why?_

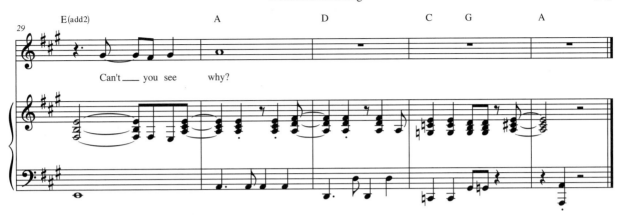

Can't __ you see   why?

Supersized

**Lyrics by
Jodi Picoult**

Music by
Ellen Wilber

May-be his e - go is what's o - ver - grown.___
Noth-ing they say can bring you to your knees.___

If the words___ of some Ne - an - der - thal___ make it hard - er to keep walk-ing tall,

___ just kneel down___ and look 'em in the eyes.___ Say you're sup - er - sized!

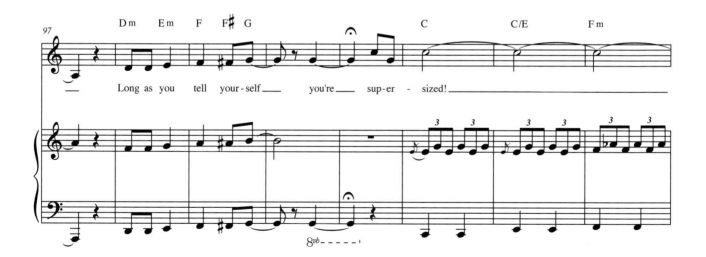

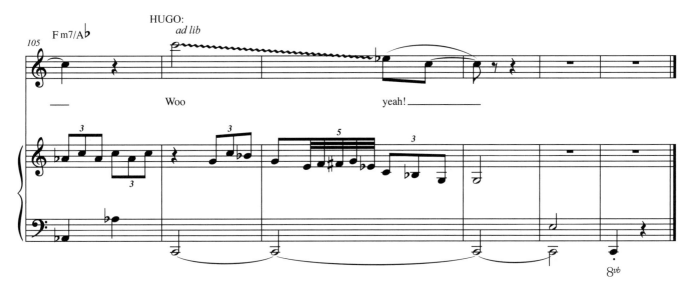

Queen of Mean

Lyrics by
Jodi Picoult

Music by
Ellen Wilber

Vocal

When I was a girl not so long a-go, my
say I took my bro-ther's king - dom. I

Piano

Ped.

bro - ther and I had a spat. My mo - ther ad - vised, I a - po - lo - gized, and
rath - er pre - fer the word "STOLE." That crash that he had? Well, gol - ly, my bad! But

then I set fire to his fav-orite cat. They thought I would out-grow my nast-y tricks,
world do - mi - na-tion's a loft-y goal. The cit - i - zens may nev-er love__ me,

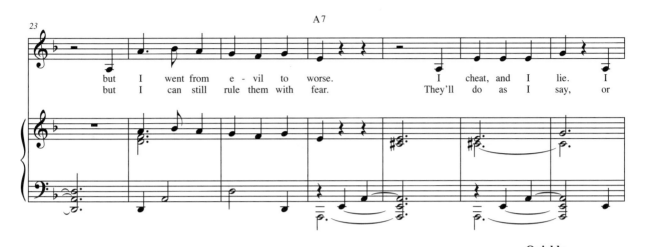

but I went from e - vil to worse.   I cheat, and I lie.   I
but I can still rule them with fear.   They'll do as I say,   or

make peo - ple cry.   Ho - ney, it's true: bad girls fin - ish first.   I'm a down-pour
may - be one day, it's pos - si - ble that they might dis - ap - pear.   I'm a rip a -

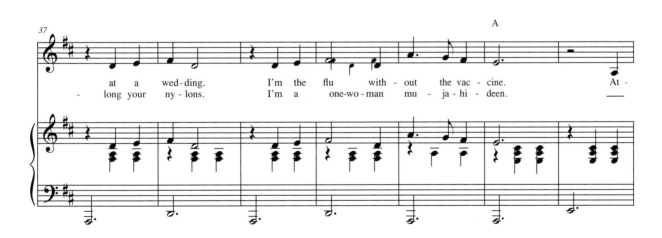

at a wed - ding.   I'm the flu with - out the vac - cine.   At -
- long your ny - lons.   I'm a one-wo - man mu - ja - hi - deen.

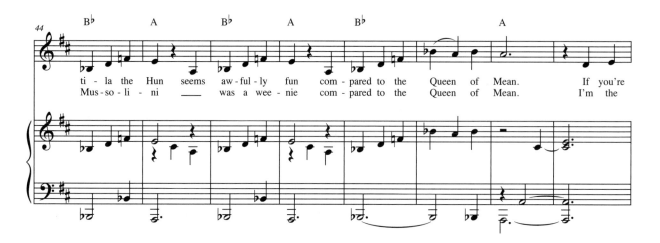

ti - la the Hun seems aw-ful-ly fun com - pared to the Queen of Mean. If you're
Mus-so-li-ni ___ was a wee-nie com - pared to the Queen of Mean. I'm the

thirst-y in the des - ert, you can bet that I'm a salt - ine. Cru -
sip of milk that's so - ur. I'm a platter of li - ma beans. George

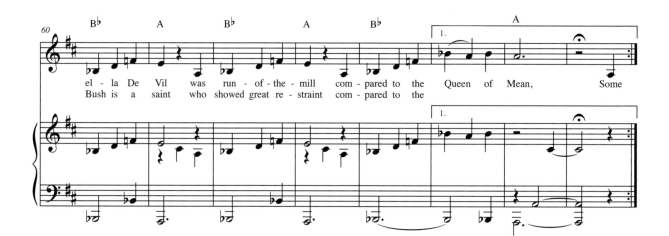

el - la De Vil was run - of - the - mill com - pared to the Queen of Mean, Some
Bush is a saint who showed great re - straint com - pared to the

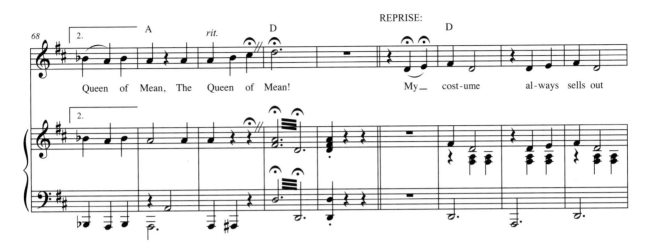

REPRISE:

Queen of Mean, The Queen of Mean! My cost-ume al-ways sells out

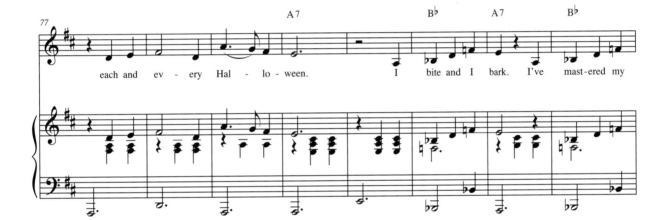

each and ev-ery Hal - lo-ween. I bite and I bark. I've mast-ered my

snark be - cause I'm the Queen of Mean, The Queen of MEAN!!!!

A Girl Like Me

Lyrics by
Jodi Picoult

Music by
Ellen Wilber

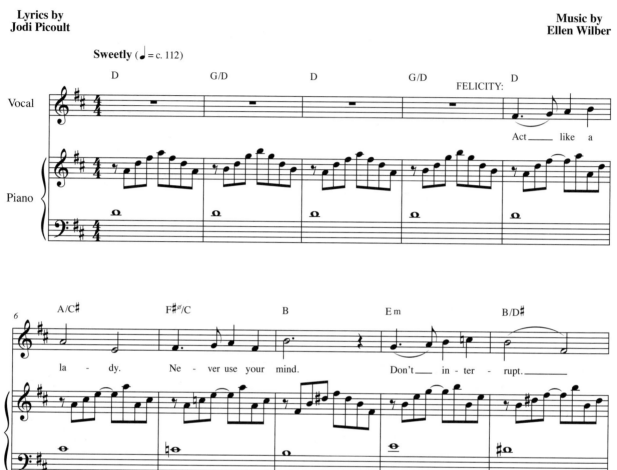

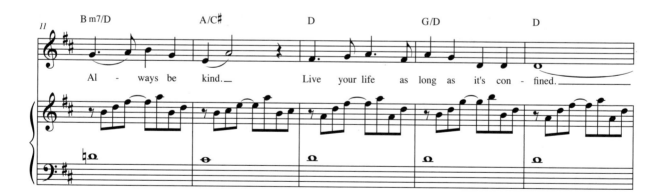

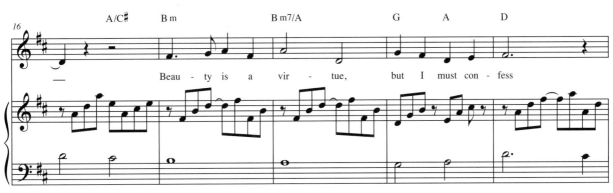

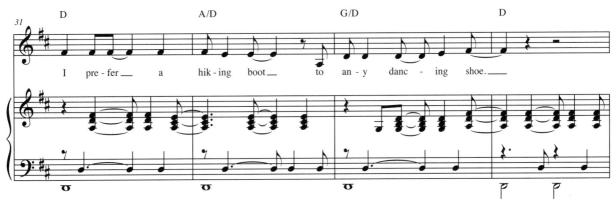

A Girl Like Me

I will tell my - self there's got to be some - one

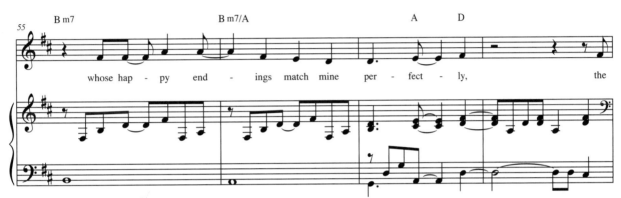

whose hap - py end - ings match mine per - fect - ly, the

kind of guy who wants a girl like me.

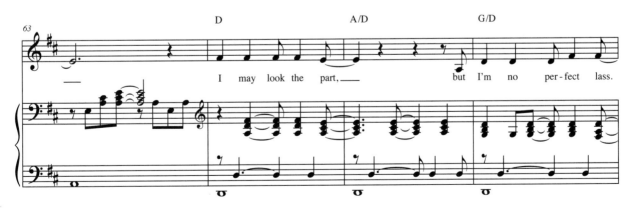

I may look the part, but I'm no per - fect lass.

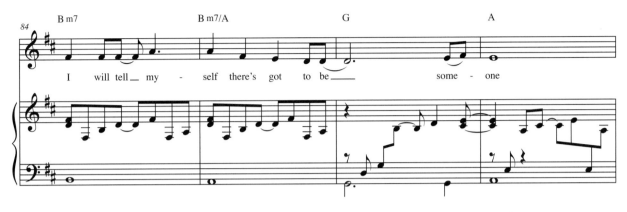

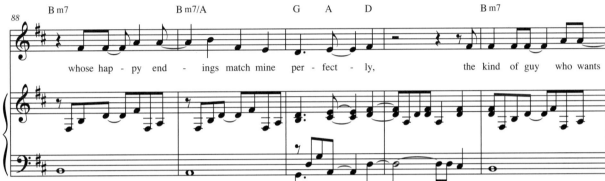

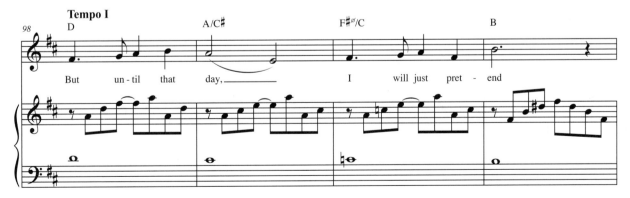

A Girl Like Me

that I could be_____ the per-fect girl - friend, though I know I'll

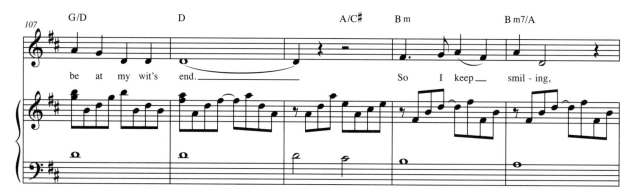

be at my wit's end._____ So I keep__ smil - ing,

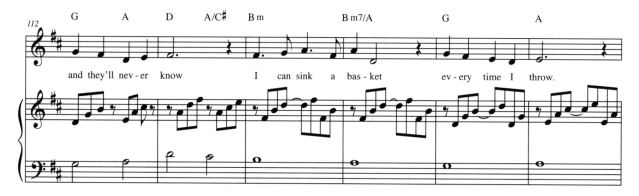

and they'll nev-er know I can sink a bas-ket ev-ery time I throw.

Where's the guy who wants a girl like me? Like me._____

Happily Never After

**Lyrics by
Jodi Picoult**

Music by
Ellen Wilber

Charm - ing leaves his stock - ings on __ the ground, __ and

nev - er puts the toi - let seat back down. That

wav - y head of hair? __ Guess what, it's a tou - pee! __ I'll take

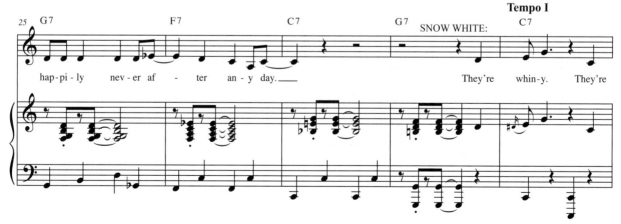

Tempo I

SNOW WHITE:

hap-pi-ly nev-er af - ter an-y day. __ They're whin-y. They're

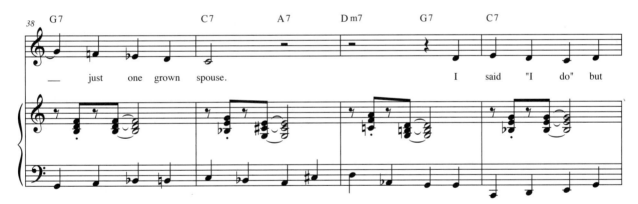

Happily Never After

a guy who snores all night when we're in bed.___ He

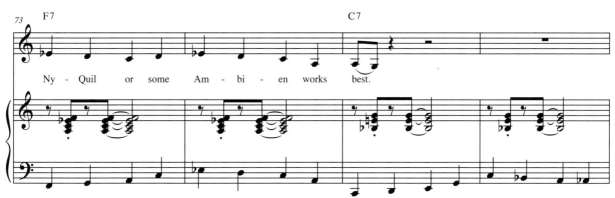

does - n't see I need a good___ night's rest.___ Some

Ny - Quil or some Am - bi - en works best.

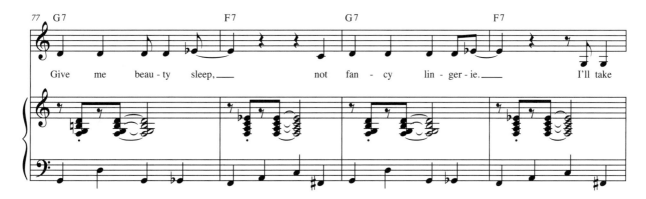

Give me beau - ty sleep,___ not fan - cy lin - ger - ie.___ I'll take

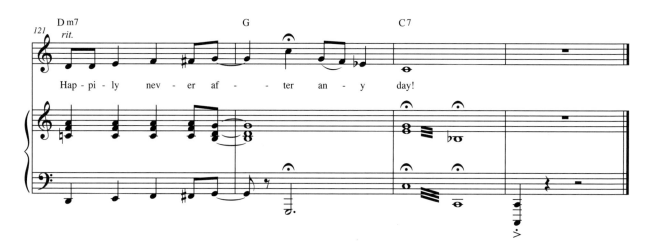

Perfect Couple

Lyrics by
Jodi Picoult

Music by
Ellen Wilber

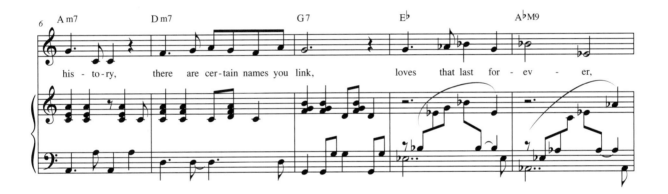

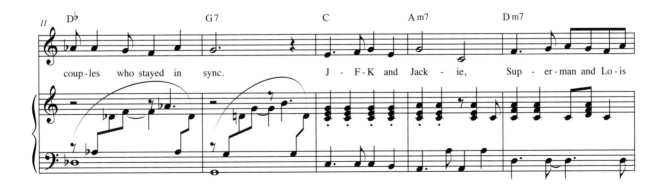

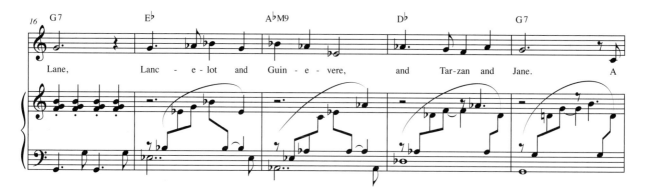

Lane, Lanc - e - lot and Guin - e - vere, and Tar - zan and Jane. A

coup - le of kis - ses, a cou - ple of dates, a cou - ple of whis - pers, a cou - ple soul mates. If on - ly I knew how to

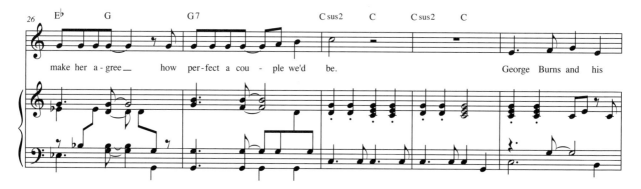

make her a - gree__ how per - fect a cou - ple we'd be. George Burns and his

Grac - ie, Ro - me - o and Jul - i - et, Hep - burn and her Tra - cy,

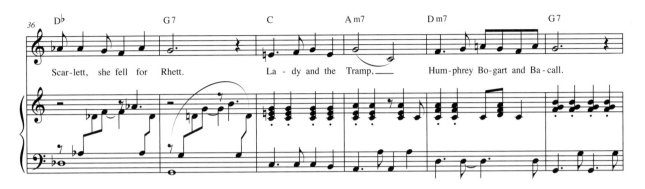

Scar-lett, she fell for Rhett. La - dy and the Tramp,___ Hum-phrey Bo-gart and Ba-call.

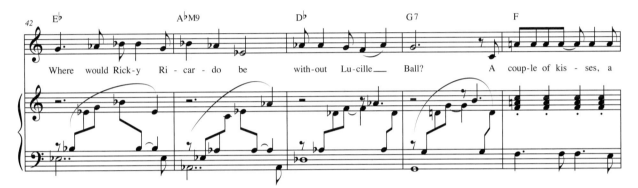

Where would Rick-y Ri - car - do be with-out Lu-cille___ Ball? A coup-le of kis - ses, a

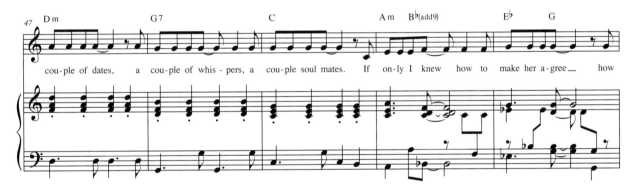

couple of dates, a cou-ple of whis - pers, a cou-ple soul mates. If on-ly I knew how to make her a-gree___ how

If I could get her to listen to me, I'd say this one thing: We could be Mark Antony and Cleopatra, but without the part at the end where everyone dies.

per-fect a cou - ple we'd be.

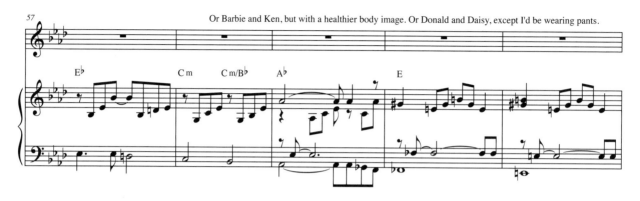

Or Barbie and Ken, but with a healthier body image. Or Donald and Daisy, except I'd be wearing pants.

Oh, well, you know what I mean, right? I love you!

Mick - ey with-out Min - nie   is   just wrong, to say the

least.   What's Bert with-out   Er - nie,   Beau-ty with-out the   Beast?

Sieg - fried needs his Roy._____   Who   is   Bon-nie with-out Clyde?   Where   would Ho - mer

Simp - son   be   if   Marge   were   not   his   bride?   A   coup - le   of   kis - ses,   a

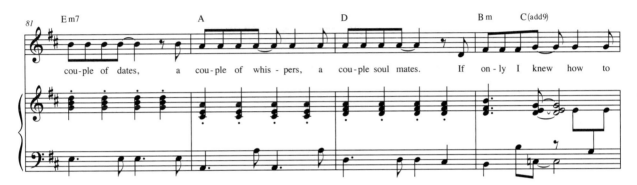

cou - ple   of   dates,   a   cou - ple   of   whis - pers,   a   cou - ple   soul   mates.   If   on - ly   I   knew   how   to

make   her   a - gree____   that   we   could   go   down____   in   hist - o - ry.____

Wish   there's   a   way   I   could   get   her   to   see   how   per - fect   a   cou - ple   we'd   be.

The Words I Can't Say

Lyrics by
Jodi Picoult

Music by
Ellen Wilber

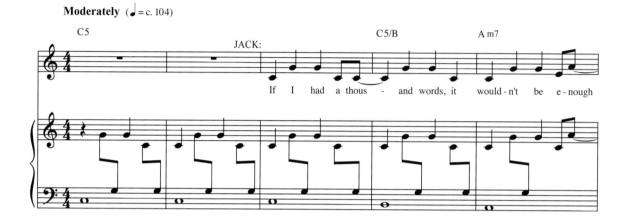

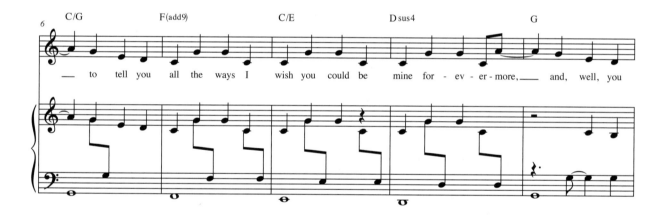

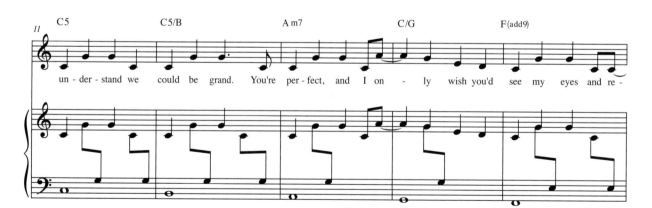

The Words I Can't Say

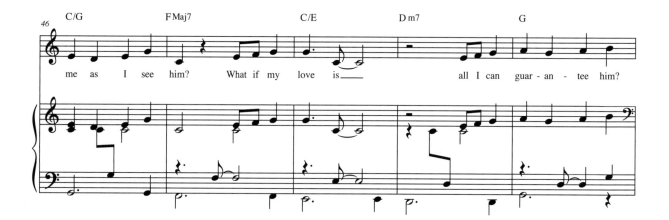

The Words I Can't Say

I'd tell you that you're part of me,___ a piece I did-n't ev — en

Could I have been so wrong? Is it as sim - ple___

would - n't be e - nough___ to tell you all the ways I wish you could be

know till now was___ lost. If you would on - ly hear___

as find - ing the one you long for? What if he looks up?___

mine for - ev - er-more,___ and, well, you un - der - stand we could be grand. You're

how much I hold you dear to___ me, how much I wish that you___ could

Could he see me as I see him? What if my love is___

per - fect, and I on - ly wish you'd see my eyes and re - a - lize___ how

see me as I am. Did - n't be - lieve___ in hap - py end - ings, did-n't care.

all I can guar - an - tee him? Did - n't be - lieve___ in hap - py end - ings, did-n't care.

long I've wait - ed now to kiss you. Did - n't be - lieve___ in hap - py end - ings, did-n't care.

The Words I Can't Say

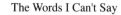

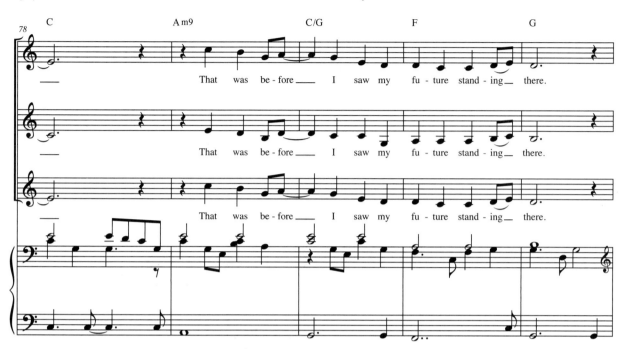

That was be-fore___ I saw my fu-ture stand-ing___ there.

That was be-fore___ I saw my fu-ture stand-ing___ there.

That was be-fore___ I saw my fu-ture stand-ing___ there.

ALL:

Ev-er-y night when I close my eyes, you're in my arms. Ev-er-y night I

hope that my dreams might soon come true. But then I wake and see there's no one

here with me. Ev - ery day, an - y - way, I will keep on wait - ing here for you.

Royal Ball

Lyrics by
Jodi Picoult

Music by
Ellen Wilber

Won - der if they'll spike the cran - ber - ry punch.
Would - n't that be____ quite a sight to be - hold?

Won - der if I'll____ get to
Won - der if I'll____ cut the

dance with the queen. Can't wait to see and to be seen!
rug with the prince. Can't wait to drop a coup - le hints!

The style!   The smile!

Royal Ball

The face!   Your Grace!   The dress!   Suc-cess!

I've al-ways thought I'd make great roy-al-ty, ___

graft-ed right on - to that fam-i-ly tree. A turn on the dance floor, a few fan-cy spins;

this could be how___ it all be-gins! Fast-en your fin - est dia-monds, i-ron your gown.

We're get-ting read - y for a night on the town. Danc-ing and sing - ing in that big roy-al hall.

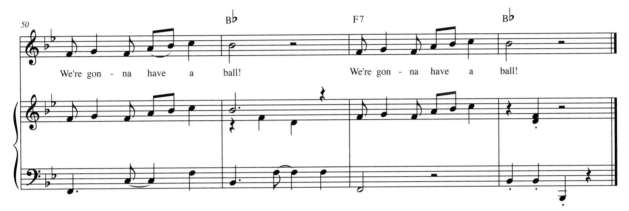

We're gon - na have a ball! We're gon - na have a ball!

Scary Forest Music

Music by
Ellen Wilber

The Hunt Song

Lyrics by
Jodi Picoult

Music by
Ellen Wilber

GROUP 1:

Grab a pitch-fork. Grab a rake. Grab what-ev-er you can take. Time to fight, for heav-en's sake, to-

night. We are stand-ing side by side. Can-not be pre-oc-cu-pied. We will not be ter-ri-fied to-

The Hunt Song

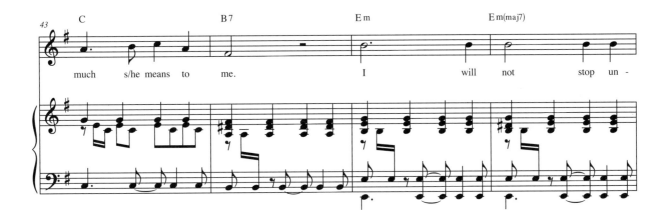

much s/he means to me. I will not stop un -

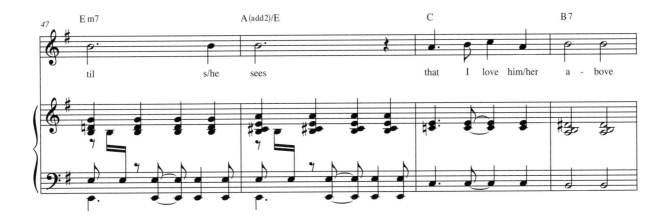

til s/he sees that I love him/her a - bove

all.

GROUP 1:
Grab a pitch-fork. Grab a rake. Grab what-ev-er you can take. Turn to fight, for heav-en's sake, to-

GROUP 2:
We will hunt the gi - - - -

JACK & LUNA:
Now at last a gold - - en op - por - tun - i -

night. We are stand-ing side by side. Can-not be pre-oc-cu-pied. We will not be ter-ri-fied to-

ant. We will hunt the gi - - -

ty to show the one I love how much s/he means to

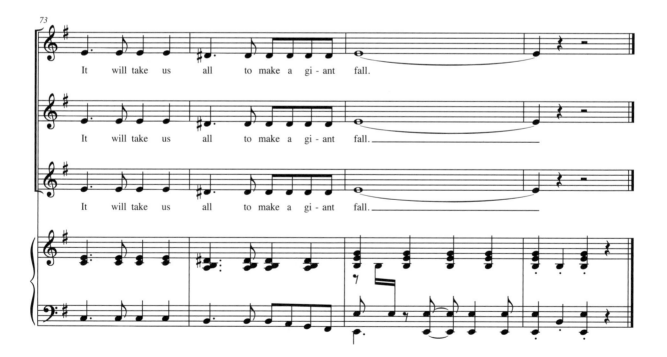

Home Sweet Home

Lyrics by
Jodi Picoult

Music by
Ellen Wilber

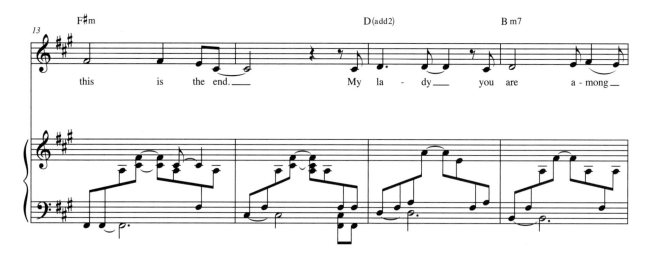

this   is   the   end.___   My   la - dy___   you   are   a - mong___

friends.   JEAN-CLAUDE
                                                                        & THREE BEARS:

                                                                        Though we

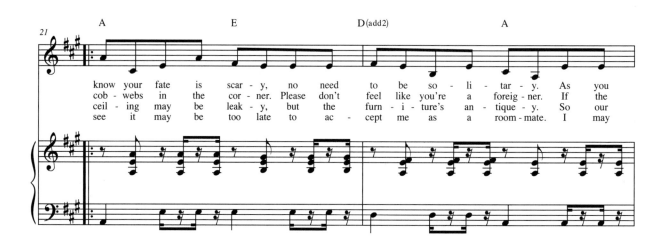

know   your   fate   is   scar - y,   no   need   to   be   so - li - tar - y.   As   you
cob - webs   in   the   cor - ner.   Please   don't   feel   like   you're   a   foreig - ner.   If   the
ceil - ing   may   be   leak - y,   but   the   fur - ni - ture's   an - tique - y.   So   our
see   it   may   be   too   late   to   ac - cept   me   as   a   room - mate.   I   may

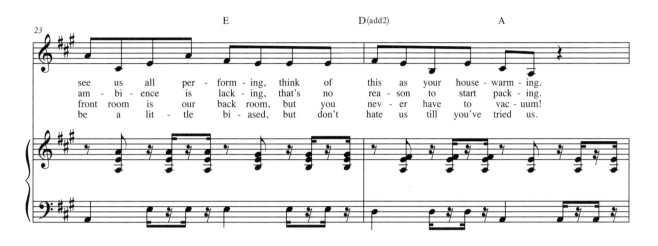

see us all per - form - ing, think of this as your house - warm - ing.
am - bi - ence is lack - ing, that's no rea - son to start pack - ing.
front room is our back room, but you nev - er have to vac - uum!
be a lit - tle bi - ased, but don't hate us till you've tried us.

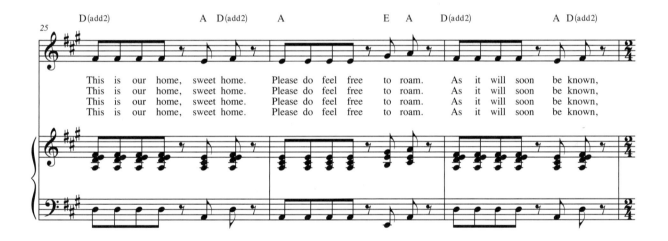

This is our home, sweet home. Please do feel free to roam. As it will soon be known,
This is our home, sweet home. Please do feel free to roam. As it will soon be known,
This is our home, sweet home. Please do feel free to roam. As it will soon be known,
This is our home, sweet home. Please do feel free to roam. As it will soon be known,

Home sweet home! So there's
Home sweet home! So our
Home sweet
Home sweet

Home   sweet   home!

It's Lonely at the Top

**Lyrics by
Jodi Picoult**

**Music by
Ellen Wilber**

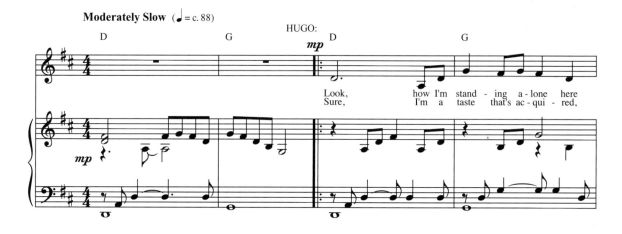

Moderately Slow (♩ = c. 88)

HUGO:

Look, how I'm stand - ing a - lone here
Sure, I'm a taste that's ac - qui - red,

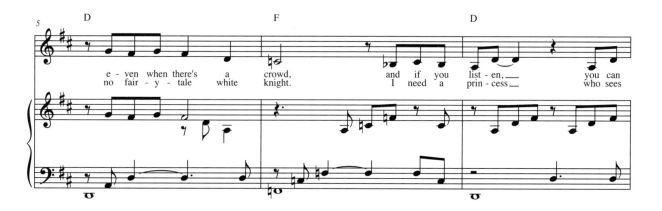

e - ven when there's a crowd, and if you list - en,___ you can
no fair - y - tale white knight. I need a prin - cess___ who sees

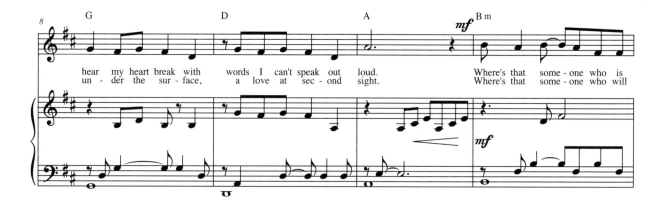

hear my heart break with words I can't speak out loud. Where's that some - one who is
un - der the sur - face, a love at sec - ond sight. Where's that some - one who will

long o - ver - due, that fine kind of love that won't stop?
try some - thing new? No need to com - par - i - son shop.

Here, I've been wait - ing a life - time. It's lone - ly at the top.
Here, I've been wait - ing a life - time. It's lone - ly at the

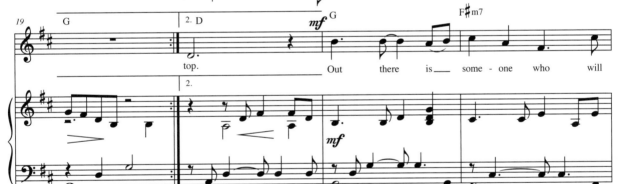

top.

Out there is__ some - one who will

love me just for me. Out there is a fu - ture full of pos - si - bil - i -

It's Lonely at the Top

Disenchanted

**Lyrics by
Jodi Picoult**

**Music by
Ellen Wilber**

Disenchanted

Disenchanted

Disenchanted

Driving Me Crazy

**Lyrics by
Jodi Picoult**

**Music by
Ellen Wilber**

Driving Me Crazy

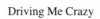

The PC Song

**Lyrics by
Jodi Picoult**

Music by
Ellen Wilber

The PC Song

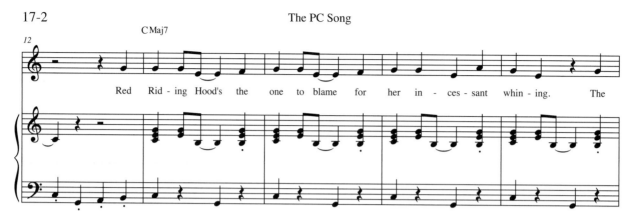

Red Rid - ing Hood's the one to blame for her in - ces - sant whin - ing. The

Big Bad Wolf was simp - ly fond of int - er - spe - cies din - ing. "What big teeth you

have," Red said, ac - cord - ing to the fa - ble. Should have said the wolf was orth - o -

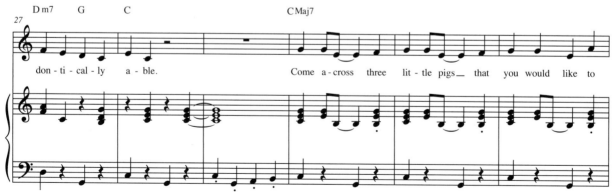

don - ti - cal - ly a - ble. Come a - cross three lit - tle pigs_ that you would like to

greet. Re - fer to them in - stead as the Oth - er White Meat.

Moth - er Hub - bard now is chron - o - log - i - cal - ly gift - ed. Sev - en dwarfs in -

sist they're on - ly vert - i - cal - ly un - lift - ed. A hur - ri - cane's a

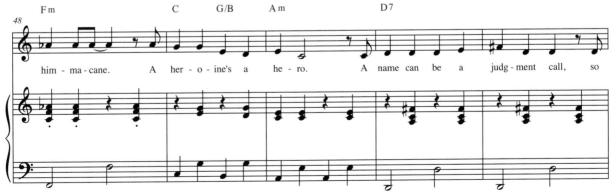

him - ma - cane. A her - o - ine's a he - ro. A name can be a judg - ment call, so

The PC Song

make sure that you're clear, oh. It's al - ways hard to find a word on which we all a -

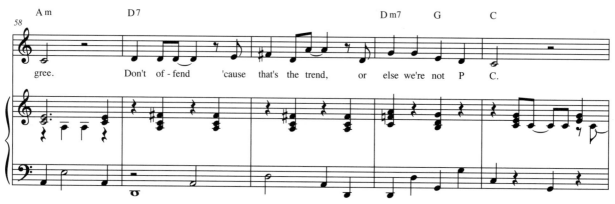

gree. Don't of - fend 'cause that's the trend, or else we're not P C.

Now we know that Cin - der - el - la just mis - un - der - stood. The

e - vil____ step - moth - er has po - ten - tial to be good. She's not the on - ly

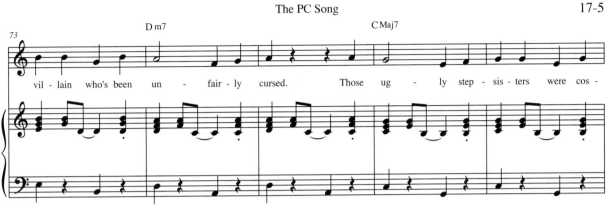

vil - lain who's been un - fair - ly cursed. Those ug - ly step - sis - ters were cos -

met - i - cally di - verse. Jack Sprat's wife was nev - er fat, __ just

dif - fer - ent - ly weight - ed. Sleep - ing Beau - ty's cer - tain she was med - i - cally se -

dat - ed. Am - phi - bi - an A - mer - i - can's the new term for Frog Prince. And

The PC Song

Gold - i - locks, she's not a blonde, her hair just some-times glints. A hur - ri - cane's a him - ma - cane. A her - o - ine's a he - ro. A name can be a judg - ment call, so make sure that you're clear, oh. It's al - ways hard to find a word on which we all a - gree.

Don't of - fend 'cause that's the trend, or else we're not P

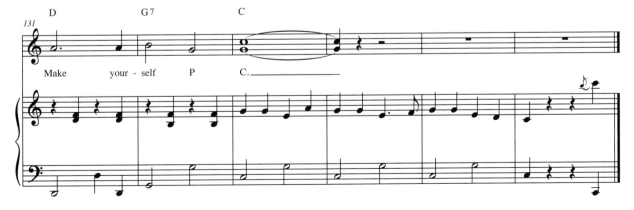

Driving Me Crazy (reprise)

Lyrics by
Jodi Picoult

Music by
Ellen Wilber

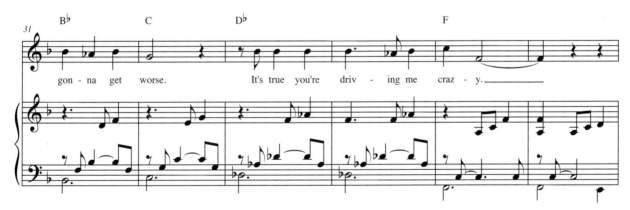

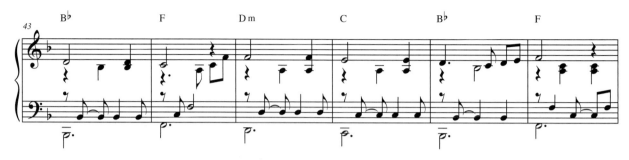

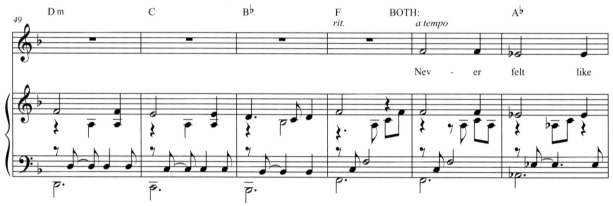

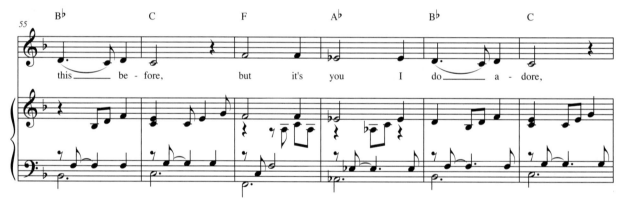

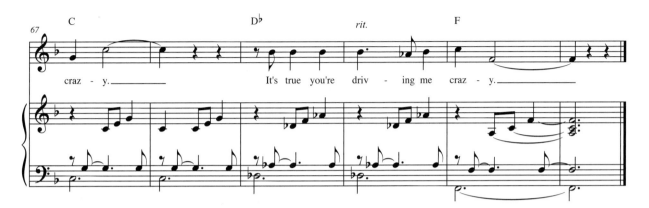

If Mama Were Normal

**Lyrics by
Jodi Picoult**

**Music by
Ellen Wilber**

If Mama Were Normal

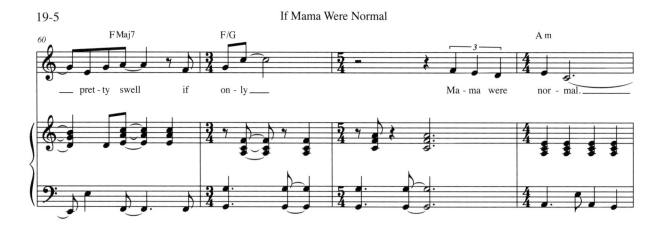

Once in a Blue Moon

Lyrics by
Jodi Picoult

Music by
Ellen Wilber

Once in a Blue Moon

It's gon-na hit you from be-hind. It's gon-na sweep you off your feet.

You lose your heart and lose your mind. That some-one spe-cial that you meet

once in___ a blue moon.

VERSE 1:

If you___ are cer-tain you___ are

lost and on___ your own, out there is some-one else___ who al-so feels a-lone.

Once in a Blue Moon

Jodi Picoult is the author of seventeen bestselling novels, including the #1 *New York Times* best-sellers *House Rules*, *Handle with Care*, *Nineteen Minutes*, and *My Sister's Keeper*. She is the codirector for the Trumbull Hall Troupe, a teen theater troupe whose proceeds go to charity. She lives in New Hampshire with her husband and children. Visit her at www.jodipicoult.com.

Jake van Leer, a high school senior, is one of the founding members of the Trumbull Hall Troupe. He has raised more than $40,000 for charity in his role as business manager for the troupe, and has performed in every show. He participates in multiple vocal and theater ensembles, and was selected for the NH All-State Music festival. Jake has performed at Notre Dame Cathedral and Carnegie Hall. He lives in New Hampshire.

Ellen Wilber is a teacher and musician with more than twenty-five years of experience introducing children to music. She is a member of the Cardigan Mountain Tradition, a bluegrass band, and the founder of a long-running kids' summer theater program. She is the music director for the Trumbull Hall Troupe, for which she has composed more than one hundred songs. She also composed and performed the music that will be featured in Picoult's 2011 novel, *Sing You Home*. Ellen lives in New Hampshire.